W9-BNA-259

CAREERS

F O R

SELF-STARTERS
& Other
Entrepreneurial Types

Blythe Camenson

VGM Career Horizons
a division of *NTC Publishing Group*
Lincolnwood, Illinois USA

Library of Congress Cataloging-in-Publication Data

Camenson, Blythe.
   Careers for self-starters and other entrepreneurial types / by
Blythe Camenson.
      p.   cm.
   Includes bibliographical references (p.).
   ISBN 0-8442-4329-9 (alk. paper).—ISBN 0-8442-4330-2 (pbk.:
alk. paper)
    1. New business entreprises—Management.   2. Small business—
Management.   3. Self-employed.   I. Title.
HD62 . 5 . C35   1996
658' .041—dc20   96-27791
                                                         CIP

Published by VGM Career Horizons, a division of NTC Publishing Group
4255 West Touhy Avenue
Lincolnwood (Chicago), Illinois 60646-1975, U.S.A.
© 1997 by NTC Publishing Group. All rights reserved.
No part of this book may be reproduced, stored in a retrieval
system, or transmitted in any form or by any means,
electronic, mechanical, photocopying, or otherwise,
without the prior permission of NTC Publishing Group.
Manufactured in the United States of America.

Dedication

To Marshall Cook, who knows how to get me started and keep me going.

Contents

About the Author   vii

Acknowledgments   ix

CHAPTER ONE
Opportunities for Self-Starters   1

CHAPTER TWO
Dream Schemes   7

CHAPTER THREE
Service Industry Careers   38

CHAPTER FOUR
Careers for Performers   58

CHAPTER FIVE
Freelance Writing   70

CHAPTER SIX
The Organizer   95

APPENDIX A
Professional Associations   109

APPENDIX B
Recommended Reading   113

About the Author

Blythe Camenson was a self-starter before she'd ever heard of the term. She put herself through college, then years later got on a plane bound for Saudi Arabia. She worked in various Persian Gulf countries for almost eight years. After being evacuated from Baghdad in 1990, she began a career as a freelance writer, then founded Fiction Writer's Connection, a membership organization formed to help new writers improve their craft and get published.

She is also a full-time writer of career books. Her main concern is helping job seekers make educated choices. She firmly believes that with enough information, readers can find long-term, satisfying careers. To that end, she researches traditional as well as unusual occupations, talking to a variety of professionals about what their jobs are really like. In all of her books, she includes first-hand accounts from people who can reveal what to expect in each occupation.

Blythe Camenson was educated in Boston, earning her BA in English and psychology from the University of Massachusetts and her MEd in counseling from Northeastern University.

In addition to *Careers for Self-Starters*, she has written several other books for VGM Career Horizons:

Career Portraits: Travel

Career Portraits: Writing

Career Portraits: Nursing

Career Portraits: Firefighting

Careers for History Buffs

Careers for Plant Lovers

Careers for Health Nuts

Careers for Mystery Buffs

Great Jobs for Communications Majors

On the Job: Real People Working in Health Care

On the Job: Real People Working in Service Businesses

Opportunities in Museums

Opportunities in Teaching English to Speakers of Other Languages

Acknowledgments

The author would like to thank the following self-starters for providing information about their careers:

Jim Anderson Anderson Glass Arts
      Boston, Massachusetts

Tom Bernardin Author
      The Ellis Island Immigrant Cookbook
      New York, New York

Matthew Carone Carone Gallery
      Fort Lauderdale, Florida

Dana Cassell Cassell Network of Writers
      North Stratford, New Hampshire

Frank Cassisa Certified personal trainer
      Boca Raton, Florida

Jeff Donnelly Tour guide
      Art Deco District
      Miami Beach, Florida

Tom Doyle   Palmetto Carriage Works
      Charleston, South Carolina

Connie Gay   Producer
      MurderWatch Mystery Theater
      Orlando, Florida

Robert Haehle Freelance garden writer
      Fort Lauderdale, Florida

Steve Herrell Herrell's Ice Cream
      Northampton, Massachusetts

David Hirsch	Moosewood Restaurant Ithaca, New York
Way Hoyt	Arborist Tree Trimmers and Associates, Inc. Fort Lauderdale, Florida
David Kaufelt	Key West Walking Tour Key West, Florida
Robin Landry	Esthetician Coral Springs, Florida
Al Mendoza	Keepsake Flowers and Gifts Dolton, Illinois
Adam Perl	Pastimes Ithaca, New York
Mary Ptak	The Stock Exchange Wilton Manors, Florida
Jim Ridolfi	Auctioneer Aspon Trading Company Troy, Pennsylvania
Roger Schmidt	18 Gardner Street Inn Nantucket, Massachusetts
Rosalind Sedacca	Advertising copywriter Lake Worth, Florida
Michael Silvestri	Hair stylist/salon owner Hollywood, Florida
Carol Stull	Grower Finger Lakes Organic Growers Cooperative, Inc. Ithaca, New York
Joyce Sweeney	Young adult writer Coral Springs, Florida
Nancy Yost	Literary agent Lowenstein Associates, Inc. New York, New York

Opportunities for Self-Starters

M any people dream of being their own boss. They fantasize about any number of enterprises: converting an old home to an inn or bed-and-breakfast, collecting antiques and opening up a shop in which to sell them, working in their own artist's studio, putting a green thumb to use in their own floral shop or nursery, opening a restaurant, or writing a book and seeing it published.

Self-starters go beyond dreaming. They plan a business or project, implement those plans, and, if all goes well, reap the benefits. How do they do it? There's no set formula for success, but self-starters share many of the same characteristics and take many of the same steps to get their enterprises off the ground.

In *Careers for Self-Starters* you will meet two dozen entrepreneurs, people who had a dream and made it come true. You will learn how each self-starter got going, obtained the necessary expertise, acquired financing, and made his or her business succeed. You will hear what pitfalls to avoid, and you'll come away with some sound advice for proceeding in similar enterprises.

Most importantly, *Careers for Self-Starters* is a book about ideas. You will learn about some traditional enterprises, some not-so-traditional ones, and some you might never have thought of. The ideas within these pages will spark other ideas or inspire spin-offs and twists on tried-and-true ones.

But first, let's see if you've got what it takes.

Self-Starter or Dreamer?

Dreamers are creative, imaginative, and innovative people. They fantasize about what could be, perhaps indulging in utopian visions of the perfect dream quest. They are romantics, idealists, and often delightful companions and friends. But unless they possess a few additional qualities, dreamers they will stay.

Self-starters dream. They're imaginative and creative, too. But they are also go-getters, independent individuals ready to turn their dreams into reality. They're willing to take risks and are not afraid to blaze their own trails. Some are even mavericks, standing out from the crowd, carving out a unique niche for themselves.

Take this short quiz and see if you're a dreamer or a self-starter.

	True	False
1. I've lived in various cities, even traveled or worked abroad.	___	___
2. It's easy for me to pick up the phone and call someone I don't know.	___	___
3. If I were my own boss, I could work only three or four days a week if I wanted to.	___	___
4. I have a sound source of financing and won't have to worry about expenses for the first year or two.	___	___
5. I expect to get rich beyond my wildest dreams.	___	___
6. I never plan ahead. I prefer to be spontaneous.	___	___
7. I'm always late, I can never find my keys, and I sure could use a good secretary to keep me organized.	___	___
8. Tax forms and spreadsheets scare the pants off me, but I muddle through.	___	___
9. I leave computers to the other guys.	___	___
10. Good contacts and luck is all it takes. I have a spot on the fast track.	___	___

Let's tally up. The ideal responses are as follows:

1. **True.** Packing up and moving to a new place takes a certain kind of courage, not unlike that involved with starting a new business.

2. **True.** Entrepreneurs often have to make a lot of cold calls, for publicity, information, and myriad other reasons.

3. **False.** Independent business owners usually work more hours than the average person employed by someone else. Seven-day work weeks are not unusual; for some, they're the norm.

4. **True.** A new business can take anywhere from one to five years to start showing a profit. It's important to have a source of income to take care of expenses during that time.

5. **False.** Although you might become rich—some do—starting out with that expectation is setting yourself up for disappointment, even failure.

6. **False.** Starting a new venture and keeping it going takes lots of planning. If you don't, it's like taking a trip without a roadmap. How will you end up where you hope to be, if you don't even know where you're going?

7. **False.** Good secretaries are expensive to hire. Most new entrepreneurs find they must wear a lot of different hats. Organizational skills are very important. Being a good juggler helps, too.

8. **False.** A solid business background is crucial to the success of any enterprise. Muddling through won't cut it.

9. **False.** Being computer literate is an essential skill to have in this day and age.

10. **False.** By now you've probably figured out that luck, although occasionally coming into play for the . . . well, the lucky ones . . . has little to do with success.

How did you do? Eighty to 100 percent marks you as a self-starter. Anything below, and you're still dreaming! In any event, read on. All self-starters began as dreamers.

The Finances Involved

Do you need to be rich to start your own business? It certainly helps. But although several of the enterprises profiled in the pages to come required substantial backing to get off the ground, others were started on a shoestring.

It's nice to have a fat bank account, but more important to have a good credit history—or a rich uncle. See how others managed it; it might help you figure out what to do.

Ideas, Ideas, Ideas

You're probably a first-time entrepreneur itching to go out on your own. You have some capital behind you, some business know-how, and the whole world out there to conquer. But what kind of enterprise should you venture into? That depends, of course, on your interests, skills, and prior experience. Let's have a taste of what's to come and see what ideas it might ignite for you.

Dream Schemes

Who hasn't dreamed of opening a bed-and-breakfast or creating a national fad? We'll meet the operator of an historic inn on Nantucket Island; a couple of collectors who finally had to clear out their attics and garages; a man who thinks buses and cars are old-fashioned; another man who knows how to say it with flowers; an acclaimed stained-glass artist who's made a name for himself; and a man who wanted to recreate a childhood experience producing homemade ice cream.

Service Industry Careers

In today's economy, service businesses are more and more the way to go. Offer to do something for another person or company that they can't do for themselves, and you'll find scores of avenues to pursue. But it's a broad highway, covering everything from hair care, personal training, and tracing family histories to plant-sitting and tree-trimming. You'll get some ideas from Chapter Three, then narrow the field down for yourself.

Careers for Performers

If you're comfortable performing in front of others, if public speaking comes naturally to you, and if you thrive on the response of a receptive audience, then here's where you'll find a few ideas to put you on the stage—so to speak.

Freelance Writing

Ah, the writer's life—being your own boss, working at home (in your bathrobe, no less), setting your own hours. From freelancer to novelist to literary agent, learn about the different writing fields you can enter and how to go about making a success of it.

The Organizer

Dreamers hope to find a club or organization to join that matches their interests; self-starters see the need and start their own. Learn how a successful collective is started, how to form an association or organize a seminar business—all careers for highly organized individuals.

There are literally thousands and thousands of ideas for self-starter careers. Just look around you; every Wendy's, every Kinko's, every Sam's Club or Costco, every boutique or bookstore was started by someone with a dream. Think back to hula hoops and happy faces. These too were started by dreamers who weren't afraid to move on to self-starter status. Certainly there's room for one more pet rock, one more published book, one more chocolate chip cookie stand. You too can join the ranks of successful entrepreneurs—all you have to do is stop dreaming and start moving.

For More Information

In addition to all the profiles and career details contained within each chapter, further information on professional associations and recommended readings for the different pursuits are listed for you in Appendices A and B, respectively.

CHAPTER TWO

Dream Schemes

Many people hold the same dream—to become self-employed; they also share many of the same dreams about how to do so. Operating a bed-and-breakfast or owning an antique store or a florist shop are just a few of the popular ventures self-starters choose to pursue.

For some, these dreams are made into reality for a first career; for others, it's a second career to look forward to, perhaps later in life, during retirement years.

Read on to see how others have fulfilled their dreams.

Operating Your Own Bed-and-Breakfast

Many entrepreneurs have been caught up in a popular movement throughout the country—restoring and refurbishing historic homes and converting them into country inns, guest houses, and bed-and-breakfast establishments.

Nantucket Island, just 30 miles off the coast of Massachusetts, is a showcase for these houses. Many of them are original Quaker homes, simple but sturdy dwellings, and perfectly preserved Georgian, Federal, and Greek Revival–style houses. Some of them are impressive mansions, the legacy of the wealth-producing whaling industry. Others are small, dollhouse-like affairs with geranium-filled planter boxes sitting below lace-curtained, leaded-glass windows.

A glimpse inside any of these homes reveals old-world mahogany antiques—carved sea chests and canopied or sleigh-back beds, many with shiny brass or even solid silver fixtures. White wicker rockers grace wooden porches, and widow walks curve around under cedar-shake roof shingles.

Tourism supports the 7,000 or so year-round residents (the summer population blossoms to near 40,000 each year), but the Nantucket Historical Association has a strong influence and strict building codes are enthusiastically adhered to by residents. Although other tourist spots are often marred by lines of fast-food stands and high-rise hotels, no intrusive golden arches or glaring neon signs are allowed on the island. Even the gas stations are disguised, their red-brick structures blending perfectly with their surroundings.

Roger and Mary Schmidt own an inn, called simply the 18 Gardner Street Inn, on Nantucket Island. The colonial-style house, which is on the historical walking tour, was originally built in 1835 by Captain Robert Joy. The sea captain took the proceeds of his last whaling excursion and built the house to retire in. Over the years, it was owned by several different families. In the 1940s the property was converted to a lodging house with six or seven rooms. The next family that purchased the inn installed bathrooms in the rooms and ran it as a bed-and-breakfast.

Restoring the Inn

The Schmidts acquired the inn in 1988. The building is a traditional square box shape with a pitched roof and an ell in the back where the kitchen was added in the late 1800s. In front there's a center door with original hand-rolled glass windows on each side. A typical Nantucket friendship staircase graces the front door, with steps on either side meeting at the landing at the top. Weathered cedar shakes (which, along with the famous Nantucket fog, help to contribute to the island's other nickname, the "Gray Lady") and a large widow's walk complete the picture of an elegant sea captain's mansion.

Spread throughout the inn's two storeys and finished third-floor attic are 12 guest rooms furnished with pencil post, canopied and four-poster beds, and antique mahogany or cherry dressers and nightstands. All of the rooms are airy; many are spacious suites, most with working fireplaces.

Roger, Mary, and their two children occupy a two-bedroom apartment in the finished basement. During the first two years they owned the inn, the Schmidts completely refurnished it. In the third and fourth years, they started doing massive restoration to the guest rooms. They took all the wallpaper down and repaired the dozens of cracks they discovered in the plaster. They upgraded the bathrooms and, keeping the period appearance to the bedrooms, repapered with pastels and satin wall coverings. They completely gutted the kitchen and replaced it with a new commercial kitchen so they could serve guests a full breakfast. And, as so often happens in old houses, they discovered a beautiful fireplace hidden for years behind one of the plaster walls. Every three years or so, the exterior of the house gets a new paint job.

One thing the Schmidts avoided was putting up new walls. They specifically chose an inn that wouldn't require massive reconstruction work. They learned from experience that putting up sheet rock can get unbelievably expensive and complicated, as does dealing with commercial building codes. Because their property had been licensed for so many years as an inn, they didn't have to be re-licensed, although they do have to get an annual license through the local building inspector.

How the Schmidts Got Started

The Schmidts are originally from Springfield in western Massachusetts. They honeymooned on Nantucket in 1977 and fell in love with the island. They started visiting three and four times a year. But when they started hunting for property to buy, it soon became obvious that the selling prices were way out of their reach.

Roger explains: "In the early eighties, property on Nantucket skyrocketed. I was in the electronics field, Mary worked in a photography lab, and the dream of owning a summer home got pushed aside because of economics. We went to the nearby island of Martha's Vineyard because we'd heard there were good buys there. We ended up finding some property there and got into the real estate business. We bought a mariner's home and completely restored it and turned it into a small, five-bedroom inn, and developed some other pieces of property there, as well. This was all happening while we were still considering Springfield as our main residence. Eventually we sold it all off and came back to Nantucket in a much better financial condition to buy our current property."

Avoiding the Pitfalls

"We had an innkeeper running 18 Gardner Street for us for two years, but we almost went bankrupt because of mismanagement," says Roger. "So, in April of 1990, we moved to the island permanently and took over running the inn. Business then took off like a cannonball. As terrible as this may sound, anybody who gets into this business and thinks he or she will succeed by serving the greatest cup of coffee and greeting every guest with a warm smile is totally wrong. It's not enough. You have to sell your property to a person on the other end of the phone. Unfortunately for that person, he doesn't know what he's getting. He can't see it and touch it. So, through written advertisements in major newspapers, such as the *Boston Globe* and the *New York Times*, and through verbal communications, you have to get across to your potential guests what your facilities are. Then, when they come, you can give them the greatest cup of coffee and the warmest smile.

"But that's still not enough. You have to understand your guests' needs and try to meet them. For example, we listened to our guests and learned that it was an inconvenience for them to have to walk downtown to pick up their rented bicycles. So we bought bicycles and provide them to our guests free of charge. We also learned that in the autumn it could be a long cold walk back from town, so that's when we made sure all our fireplaces were working. That keeps the fall business coming in. Again, we listened and learned that guests would like a little more than a muffin and coffee for breakfast. So, we got a food-service permit and offer a full meal in the morning. We also provide dockside shuttle service from the ferry to the inn, picnic baskets, beach blankets, and ice coolers. We do what we can to make our guests happy. This has helped to substantially build up our word-of-mouth referral business.

"A lot of people want to live out their romantic dream by retiring to an idyllic spot such as Nantucket and running a bed-and-breakfast. But the first major mistake they make is when they use the word 'retiring.' There's nothing retiring, or romantic, about operating an inn. You have to work very hard.

"From April 1 to November 31, my day is primarily involved with taking reservations and handling problems and delegating responsibilities to our staff of five. During the winter, we involve ourselves with marketing, and interior design and restoration. We're always busy."

The Finances Involved

"In 1988, we paid $850,000 for our historic inn, and, at the time, that was a good price." According to Roger, "The property dropped in value to $600,000 in the next two years, but now because of the restoration and the steady clientele we've built up, our property and our business is worth slightly over $1 million.

"Right now our rooms are full about 100 days of the year, and we are aiming to have full occupancy every weekend through the off-season months. The inn is an upscale one, and our high season rates are from $140 to $170 a night. But our monthly operating expenses and our mortgage payments are very high, too.

"Nantucket, of course, is a small and very expensive island. There are many areas in the country where you could pick up a small house or an established inn for around $100,000.

"Whatever the value, the trick is to have an understanding of real estate financing and to try to be a little creative. In our case, we put very little down; the owner was willing to hold back a second mortgage. Another alternative is to lease with an option to buy.

We've just done that with the property adjoining ours, and now we have five more guest rooms to book.

"But I would advise starting out with a property with just three or four guest rooms. It's a very risky business, and there's a high burnout and turnover rate. Sometimes the dream can turn into a nightmare. You can't treat it as a dream. You have to treat it as a business."

The Carriage Trade

"There's nothing better than a good mule, there's nothing worse than a bad one," says Tom Doyle, owner of the Palmetto Carriage Works, a horse- and mule-drawn carriage tour company in Charleston, South Carolina. "The thing about the bad ones, though, is that they don't hide it very well. I can spend an afternoon with a mule and know whether or not it's going to work. A horse will go by something 99 times as if it wasn't there, but on the hundredth time, the time you're not paying attention, the horse will absolutely freak out. Mules are much easier to train."

And if anyone should know the characteristics of mules, it's Tom Doyle. He has built up his tour business and now employs 28 people, owns a stable right in the heart of the city, and has 26 carriages, 2 horses, and 28 mules.

"The fellow who began the business started off with just the frame of an old farm wagon," says Tom. "He built some seats and a roof on top of it. He also had a carriage from the Jack Daniels Brewery, and he picked up a few old carriages from auctions. But they're not really built heavy-duty enough for the kind of work we use them for, and they're too small. It's hard to find an antique carriage that will carry 6 or 16 people. Because of that, we began designing our own carriages."

Tom employs one person who does nothing but build carriages. He also has a full barn staff, an office manager, a bookkeeper, a secretary, a ticket collector, and drivers who also double as grooms.

But everyone is also a licensed tour guide. "The key to doing well in the carriage business," Tom explains, "is when the business is here, you've got to be able to handle it, and when it's not here, you have to be able to get real small. We're very seasonal."

How Tom Got Started

Tom Doyle came to Charleston from Massachusetts to study at the Citadel. When he finished with his BA in history, he looked around for work he would enjoy. But most of the things he liked to do didn't pay enough money to support a family, so he was often forced to hold down two jobs. Because of this moonlighting, he discovered the Palmetto Carriage Works and started with them as a part-time carriage driver–cum–tour guide. Within a year, however, he had graduated to full-time driver and was working 60 to 70 hours a week. When the original owner decided it was time to retire, in 1982, he offered the business to Tom. "I didn't have a dime at the time," Tom admits, "but he gave me such a good deal, I was able to go out and find some other people who were willing to invest, and I put together a little group of silent partners."

But it's possible to start small in this business, Tom maintains. You don't need an office or a ticket collector or a fleet of carriages. With an investment of about $6,000 for the carriage, tack, animal, and various permits, you can position yourself in a place that's visible to tourists—outside a visitor's information center, or a popular place to stay or visit. "It's a see-and-do thing," says Tom. "The carriages themselves are the best advertising. Tourists will ask the driver, 'Hey, how do I get on one of these?' "

Making a Go of It

But to make it work you have to live the business, Tom warns. You have to be out there driving every day, making friends, and getting to know everyone. Then word of mouth will get you going.

Tom also markets his business to the big hotels in town and the meeting planners and has found his niche with large groups. "People come into town for a conference or some other event, and they might want to do an off-premises function, maybe have dinner at an historic building. I tell them, 'Well, here's what we'll do. We'll pick you up in carriages and transport you there.' "

Tom also runs a free shuttle service with his 1934 antique Ford bus. He moves his customers from the visitor's center to his starting point. "But the real bread and butter of the business is the walk-up tourist."

Tom's tours are an hour long and cover 20 blocks of the old city. Drivers provide a nonstop narration covering Charleston's history, architecture, gardens, people, and points of interest.

"As opposed to a motorized tour, our drivers can turn and talk to the people and make eye contact," Tom says. "It's a leisurely business. While you're waiting for the carriage to fill up, you chat with the passengers. To have a really great tour you need to get to know your customers. And tourists are great to deal with, because 99.9 percent of them are in a good mood. They're on vacation, after all! When I take people on a carriage tour, everyone in the city benefits, because I leave them so happy with Charleston, they're wanting to do more and to come back."

A Few Golden Rules

To have a successful business, you must love the city where you're set up, and you have to be an expert and know everything about its local history. "Good business sense is also important," Tom says, "and when you're the boss you have to monitor your drivers— the tour they give is the most important part. I occasionally pay strangers to ride and check out the drivers."

Tom is convinced that it's more than a job, it's a lifestyle. "You get to work with the animals, which I really like; you can bring your children to work; all the neighborhood kids come around the stables to help out and get free rides. You have to do a good job. You're not only representing yourself, you're representing the whole city."

Where to Find That Carriage

"If you can find an Amish settlement, you'll be able to find carriages and farm wagons for sale," Tom explains. "There are large settlements in Pennsylvania, Indiana, Ohio, and Tennessee. To help locate these settlements, write or call the state's department of tourism, and they'll be able to direct you."

Dealing in Antiques

"If you scratch a dealer, you'll find a collector underneath," reveals Adam Perl, proprietor of Pastimes, an antiques and collectibles shop in Ithaca, New York. "Many of us have gone into business just to finance our collecting habits."

Adam's own collecting habit began in the seventh grade when a classmate brought a book to school called *Cash for Your Coins*. But even if that hadn't happened, it's unlikely the collecting bug would have passed Adam by. He grew up surrounded by art and antiques; his mother is an art historian who worked at the Museum of Modern Art in New York, the Andrew Dickson White Museum at Cornell, and the Smithsonian's Hirshhorn Museum. His father was a writer, and both were serious antique collectors.

Surprisingly, Adam had never been to an auction until he was a young adult. He had just rented an unfurnished apartment when he found out about a country auction being held nearby.

"I was instantly hooked. I spent $100 and filled my van three times. I furnished my entire apartment with items left over to spare. The early seventies was a golden age of buying, when wonderful three- and four-generation estates were being broken up all over the country, but especially in the Northeast. There wasn't much of an antique market in any field then—you could buy anything for the proverbial song in those days."

With no thought of turning it into a business at that time, Adam began frequenting auctions for the fun of it. He'd go out with $5 or

$10 in his pocket and come home with treasures. "I kept doing it over and over again, until I felt I had much more than I could fit in my apartment. I realized from seeing people's setups at flea markets that they had an organized system of pricing and that they generally specialized in a particular area, such as knives or dolls. I learned that if I took the things I bought and cleaned them up a bit— polished the brass, refinished the wood, and stove-blacked the iron—that I could actually sell them for more than I had paid for them. I had my first garage sale and made a little money on it. It wasn't much of a step from that to connect up with New York City and the contacts I had there."

How Adam Got Started

Adam talked to several dealers and tried to feel out people who were sympathetic and would teach him. "At the time, the world of antiques was pretty much a mystery; there was this arcane underground where people wouldn't reveal their secrets or knowledge to anyone."

Adam found his sympathetic antique dealers at American Hurrah, which is now a well-known shop run by Joel and Kate Kopp, specializing in quilts and photographic images. "The Kopps were very forthcoming and didn't hold anything back. One thing they taught me is that you should try to double your money. You don't always do it, or sometimes you do better, but that's what you aim for. They taught me how to judge the condition of an item, and how to develop and trust your own taste. They also helped to bail me out when I made mistakes.

"I became a 'picker,' a term in the industry for a wholesaler. The picker, during his antique-hunting expeditions, tries to pick out the one great item out of the 10,000 he sees. I would actually buy retail at shops in upstate New York, perhaps finding a quilt, beautifully made and in excellent condition, for $25 to $50. I would take it to the city and sell it for double.

"The Kopps had taught me to look for the fine cotton quilts that were hand-stitched with good colors and good patterns and early nineteenth-century materials. I had bought a quilt at a garage sale for $4, but it didn't meet any of those criteria. It was thick, heavy wool, twentieth-century, rather ugly. But still, there was something about it that was really striking. It had a man's wool tanktop bathing suit stitched into it, complete with its Sears Roebuck label. I took this to New York, but the Kopps didn't think much of it. But they were always very nice to me; they bought the quilt for $12 and I was relieved. Later they turned around and were able to sell it for $50. This quilt was sold many times, and eventually ended up in the Louvre Museum in Paris, as an important example of early twentieth-century American folk art. Anybody who's been in business has made mistakes from time to time. Incidents like this can happen to the best of us."

Starting on a Shoestring

Adam opened his first shop in 1973 with just $400. A condemned high school had just been bought by an architect who remodeled it and converted it into a lively arcade of shops and boutiques called the DeWitt Building.

Adam rented what he called "an unpretentious hole-in-the-wall" for $125 a month plus one month's security. The landlord gave him some paint, and he bought a huge old machine-made oriental rug for $1. "The rug had several feet missing in the corner. I spent another dollar and bought a big overstuffed chair to cover the hole. After the $2 I spent on decor, I had $148 left for merchandise."

Adam left the business for a few years, then returned in 1978 to open his current shop, Pastimes. "This is one of the best businesses to get into on little or no capital. You don't need any particular expertise or any particular degree. You do need to have some stock and a couple of tables and table coverings. And then you can hit the flea markets. You can still find perfectly good flea markets where you can set up for $10 to $25. Later, you can graduate to a little bit higher caliber show, whose fees might be from $35 to $100. A lot of people just do shows. It's the exception, actually, having a retail shop. You're tied down and have the overhead.

"Many people get started in this business as they're heading toward retirement. They ease into it the last five or ten years of their working career, and then do it as a retirement business to supplement their pension and social security income.

"And, it's a recession-resistant business. When times are hard, antiques are a better buy than new items. People are shopping more carefully and even noncollectors who just want to get good practical furniture, tools, or gifts will turn to antiques."

Choosing Your Specialty

There are probably more than 10,000 branches in the antiques and collectibles business. You can take any particular area that interests you—whether it be local history, silver making, the history of advertising, woodworking, tools, lace making, or photographica—and turn that area into a whole specialty and a whole business. "Look for an area you love," Adam advises, "and learn more about it and concentrate in it.

"I specialize in about five or six areas I happen to have a particular love and feeling for—antique buttons, costume jewelry from the Victorian era through the forties, 1910 postcards, fountain pens, sterling silver, and antique beads. We also carry some oak furniture, glassware, and photographica. Pastimes is relatively small but it looks like a well-organized and cleaned-up flea market."

Avoiding the Pitfalls

Adam is a firm believer that in this business the less money you have the better: "I knew a young man who had inherited $50,000. This was many years ago when that was really a lot of money. He went out and bought every exquisite piece of furniture he could find. I remember at the auctions I was very jealous; he could outbid everybody. He opened up a shop with all those beautiful things, but he couldn't sell them because he'd paid too much for them.

Through experience, you have to develop knowledge of what the market will bear. There's no substitute for the actual buying and selling of merchandise to learn about the market and pricing. There are thousands of antique price guides, but this is something you can't really learn by the book. It's best to get into it gradually, go to a lot of antique shows and shops, compare prices, do your homework.

And you have to be careful about where you buy your merchandise, Adam warns. It's vital to make sure the auctioneers and dealers are reputable. "There's a great deal of dishonesty in the business," he admits. "A dealer might misrepresent an item's condition or authenticity. It's easy to get caught. Fairly recently a local dealer of questionable repute came across a big stash of mint-condition German lithographs that were reported to be from the turn of the century. We'd never seen anything like it—there are certain processes you just can't duplicate, and this was one of them. The dealers were scarfing them up for $7 to $10 a piece. We found out they were repros, but not before a lot of us got stung.

"And 10 years ago I was selling some red-colored Fiestaware, a very popular deco dinnerware made by Homer Laughlin in the thirties, forties, and fifties. It turned out to be radioactive. Some of the glazes had been made with uranium."

The Upside of the Business

Adam loves what he's doing, always chasing after the next bargain, enjoying the wonderful thrill of the hunt, that feeling you get looking for treasures and bargains. "It keeps you excited and fueled up when you're unloading your van in the cold rain, or you're stuck in the mud at an auction."

Adam Perl was hooked on collecting antiques after he'd attended his first auction. Perhaps the style of the auctioneer had something to do with it. For a look at what life is like from the other side of the gavel, you will find a profile of an auctioneer in Chapter Three.

Vintage Clothing

Most children love to play dress-up, and Mary Ptak, co-owner of the Stock Exchange, a vintage clothing shop in Fort Lauderdale, Florida, was no exception. "I wanted to spend all my time in people's attics," Mary confesses. "I was mainly interested in finding old-style clothing. When I was in college in the sixties, I would just literally knock on strangers' doors and ask them if I could clean out their attics. In those days, they were usually delighted for you to do that."

But times have changed, and people are much more aware of the treasures they might have stored away. "Gone are the days when you could pick up something for 25 cents or under," Mary says.

Mary and her partner, Carol Levin, have been in business since 1986. They were both dissatisfied with their jobs, and one day just decided to take the plunge. Carol loves the sales end of the business, dealing with the customers, and Mary satisfies her shopping urges by traveling around the country as the Stock Exchange's buyer.

Over the years, they've managed to build up an international clientele, including collectors from Japan, Germany, and England.

"Our customers are an eclectic mix of people," Mary says. "People from England and Japan have been buying up everything they can find from the fifties. Our serious collectors tend to buy clothes from the thirties through the fifties—Joan Crawford, Great Gatsby, and Garbo styles with big padded shoulders and lots of sparkly glitz. Lilli Ann suits from the forties and fifties are popular now, too. They're extremely classy looking, nipped in at the waist with flaring peplums. Some of our customers are Victorian period collectors, but most people now want the article they're buying to be useful—they want to be able to wear it. Local kids are demanding sixties and seventies garments. The kids even want the polyester nik-nik shirts from the sixties—foul-looking things, but they're popular now. The kids are always a little more savvy than the general public, and they start fashion trends with their regular street clothes. I used to be able to buy what I liked, now I have to think in terms of my customers' needs."

The Stock Exchange carries clothes ranging in price from $5 for an Indian cotton gauze blouse from the sixties to a $2,000 Schaparelli gown. It also handles rentals, outfits murder mysteries, and has supplied the costumes for several major television shows and motion pictures, including *Key West, Cape Fear*, and *Wrestling Ernest Hemingway*.

How It's Done

Mary travels all over the country to look for just the right pieces. She also has built up a network of people who ship her good finds.

"I learned what was collectible from being in the business a long time," Mary explains. "You have to have a good eye to pick what people want, and you have to change with the times—trends are constantly changing, and you can't always be buying the same things."

For anyone considering a similar business, Mary cautions that it is important to buy clothes that are in excellent condition, unless it's something that's really ancient and people would expect it to be damaged. "And you also need a huge amount of stock. When we started out we had very little, but we took consignments then, and because I'm a fanatic shopper, it didn't take long to build it up."

Mary and Carol also managed to build themselves a first-class reputation. "We make an effort to pay people what they deserve for their merchandise. It's one of the reasons we've been so successful."

The Finances Involved

The Stock Exchange is a classic example of laughing all the way to the bank. In 1986, no one would give the two women a business loan. "They didn't think we'd make it," Mary says with just a touch of righteous indignation in her voice.

The two partners recently opened another store in a popular shopping area in Fort Lauderdale. Jezebel, as they've called it, carries upscale vintage clothing, accessories, and antiques.

Mary is kept very busy with the two stores. The one thing she doesn't have time to do anymore is hunt through people's attics. These days she can hire other people to do that.

Say It with Flowers

Florists either own and operate their own shops or work in a shop owned by someone else. Self-starters choose the former route.

There are three kinds of flower shops: cash-and-carry stores, decorator shops, and service shops. Cash-and-carry stores, or merchandising stores as they are also known, sell bunches of prewrapped flowers. Generally, customers cannot order special arrangements through these shops; selections are limited to what is immediately available and on hand. Cash-and-carry shops are found in the neighborhood supermarket's flower section, at farmers' markets, or at impromptu "shops" set up in buckets alongside of the road.

Decorator shops, which are few and far between, operate as specialists, providing custom-made arrangements for important occasions such as weddings or balls. They generally do not cater to walk-in customers.

The largest percentage of florists are service florists, meaning they offer a service in addition to a product. They design, custom-make, and deliver their merchandise.

Location, Location, Location

As with any business that hopes to garner off-the-street customers, location is always the first consideration. Because flowers are considered to be more a luxury item than a necessity (although fervent plant lovers would surely argue that point), most successful florist shops are found in suburban town centers as opposed to downtown, inner-city locations. They also can do well in shopping malls.

The Skills You Need

To be a successful florist, a love of plants, although crucial, is not enough. Florists must have training in every aspect of the industry and possess strong business skills. The best preparation is gaining a combination of on-the-job experience and education.

Trainees can gain experience working part-time for retail and wholesale florists, for greenhouses and nurseries, or for cut-flower growers. With this kind of exposure, potential florists can learn about packing and unpacking; processing; shipping; propagation; cutting; seed sowing; bulb planting and potting; basic floral design; and pickup, delivery, and sales work.

While in school, students should take courses in biological sciences, math, communications, computer science, and general business, including retail store management.

Some academic and vocational institutions offer two- and four-year programs geared directly to floriculture and horticulture. Many also provide students with the opportunity for on-the-job training while they are still in school through cooperative education programs. Co-op programs place students in related business settings and, after the first year of academics, alternate semesters with work and study.

The Society of American Florists has prepared a list of colleges, universities, and postsecondary schools offering two- and four-year degree programs and technical and certificate programs. The courses cover general horticulture, ornamental horticulture, floriculture, and floral design. The society's address can be found in Appendix A.

Al Mendoza is proprietor of Keepsake Flowers and Gifts in Dolton, Illinois. He is also assistant director at the American Art Floral School in Chicago.

Al says, "I always tell any student who is coming to our school and planning on opening up a flower shop that it's great to know floral design, but it's more important to have a business degree than a floral degree. More businesses fail because they think of it as an art business rather than an actual commercial business. If someone wants to get their training through college, they should major in business with a minor in floral design.

"I can take someone off the street and teach them design," he continues. "It's very mechanical. You establish your height, your width, your depth. The art part is where the talent comes in."

Many floral designers and future florist shop owners get their training working in a florist shop, learning as they go. They also attend seminars and workshops and take courses at floral design schools. The American Floral Art School, in business for over 50 years, is one of the best known in the world. It offers an intensive three-week course, after which Al Mendoza says students will graduate as competent designers with a good understanding of the basics.

"A three-week course," Al explains, "is enough to help a student get his or her foot in the door at a flower shop. But, really, three weeks is not enough. The rest of the training comes from on-the-job experience. But it's a Catch-22 situation. It's difficult to get that first job without some sort of training. Our program helps to open the door."

During the three-week program at the American Floral Art School, students study art and mechanics. "The art is what you see in a design, the mechanics are how you put it together," Al explains. "As a teacher, I stress more the mechanics than the art. The art will come to them naturally, the colors and the choice of flowers and the mixing, but the basic foundations of design are more important, what it is you need to make this whole composition come together. In the first week we cover the seven principles of floral design: balance, accent, proportion, composition, unity, rhythm, and harmony and how they apply to funeral work. We gear the second week to using these principles and how they apply to everyday arrangements and party work. The third week we go into wedding work."

For further training, students attend seminars and workshops sponsored by local wholesalers or the American Institute of Floral Design (AIFD), which is the professional association to which floral designers strive to belong. Admission to this organization is very competitive.

The Downsides of the Job

Florists work long hours, and as Al Mendoza says, "When most people are out enjoying the various parties, you're working at them. During holiday times, most people are having fun, enjoying the festivities, but again, it's the busiest time of the year for florists. In the floral world you don't get weekends and holidays off. I can't remember the last time my family and I could share a decent holiday together—Christmas, Easter. You're working like crazy the week before, then you're so exhausted, you can't enjoy yourself."

The Finances Involved

To start a florist shop these days an initial investment of about $50,000 would be required. And, in today's economy, Al says you can expect to work eight to ten years before realizing a profit.

"It's a risk when you're dealing with perishables. People could lose a lot if they don't know how to order. If they order too much they can lose, or if they don't order enough they can lose. A typical example would be Valentine's Day. If you order too many roses, if you buy a thousand too many, you can lose thousands of dollars. But it's hard to learn how to get the ordering right. That's why it's so important to work for other florists before venturing out on your own. You need the experience."

An Artist's Dream

If you have artistic talent you might be dreaming of one day opening your own studio or gallery, a place in which to create and sell your work. Whether it's pottery or painting, sewing or stained glass, artistic self-starters can make a name for themselves and work full-time in their chosen area—without starving in an artist's garret.

The two people in this section followed their dreams and made a success of it.

Jim Anderson: Stained-Glass Artist

Over the last 20 years, Jim Anderson has established himself as a successful stained-glass artist in Boston. His studio on Tremont Street in the revitalized South End neighborhood is called Anderson Glass Arts. He attended Boston Museum School of Fine Arts and Massachusetts College of Art and graduated with a BFA and a teaching certificate.

"I started drawing and painting when I was young," says Jim. "Even in my baby book it says stuff like Jimmy is creative, Jimmy is artistic, Jimmy can draw. It's one of the areas where I got affirmation as a child.

"I found that I really loved the combination of art and architecture, as opposed to paintings that just hang on walls. I liked the fact that stained glass becomes a permanent part of a building—it becomes architectural art.

"My designs range to all kinds of styles—traditional as well as contemporary. I do handpainted glass like you see in churches, and I do styles from different periods: Victorian, Federal, Edwardian, all periods.

"Even as a kid I remember looking at church windows—just staring at them when I was in church. Little did I know that I'd be making them when I got older. I did my first church when I was 26, St. George's Greek Orthodox Church in Hyannis. Now I'm amazed at that kind of undertaking for such a young man. I remember that my colleagues in New York and other places were astounded that the commission for a church was given to such a young artist."

How Jim Got Started

"After the Boston Museum School, I went to Massachusetts College of Art to pursue a teaching certificate because I was afraid I wouldn't be able to support myself as an artist and I wanted something to fall back on," Jim explains. "But during that time, I realized that I was already actually supporting myself. I started making windows for people, and it paid my way through school.

"Commissions started coming because people saw the work I did on my own house. I own a brownstone in the South End, which is the largest Victorian neighborhood in America with over 2,000 structures intact, bowfronts and brownstones.

"I set up a workshop on the ground level of the townhouse so I'd have a place to work, then I did my doorways first. Other neighbors saw them and really loved them. Some of my neighbors were professional architects, and they asked if I'd do their doors. Then other people saw the work and it mushroomed. Over the years I've done ten or fifteen doors on my street alone, and then other people on different streets started seeing them and hiring me.

"Then, before I knew it, someone wrote an article about me in the *Boston Globe*, then in other papers; then Channel Two did a documentary on revitalizing an old art form that included my work. At that point, I started getting more and more work. I moved my studio out of my house to a more visible commercial area. I wanted to be able to keep my work on display in the windows.

"Now I have a couple of assistants—one to help me, one to do repair and restoration work. How many assistants I have depends on the economy and how much work I have. As things improve, I take on assistants, but if things drop off, I have to let them go. I always make sure there's enough work for at least myself, but now it's doing well, so I can afford to hire help.

"I like going to people's houses and making beautiful windows they really love and that I feel are appropriate for their homes. I wouldn't put a modern window in a Victorian, for example, it wouldn't be suitable.

"I meet a lot of interesting people in my work. Maybe it's because it's an unusual art form, and it's usually interesting people who want it.

"The work is fun and challenging, and I'm always learning something new. The older I get, the more complicated and sophisticated the commissions get."

The Finances Involved

"Money doesn't come in regularly, but it always seems to come in," says Jim. "Sometimes in big chunks, sometimes in little chunks. I never know when or what, but I haven't starved and I haven't not paid my bills yet."

Some Advice from Jim

"Follow your dream, listen to your gut on what to do. Visualize what you want for yourself, then slowly go toward it.

"But start slowly," he warns. "In my first studio, I made worktables out of plywood and other basic, simple things I could find. Nothing fancy or expensive, whatever I could scavenge. I've refined the space over time. "Don't spend too much as you go along, let your business build up and don't overextend yourself.

"How important the location of your studio is depends on the art form. If you're a painter, your aim would be to be shown in galleries, so it doesn't matter so much where your studio is. But for other art forms, such as stained glass, it would.

"There are cooperative buildings for artists in lots of major cities now. It's nice to work around other artists and share old warehouse space. It gives you a lot of exposure, plus it keeps you in the art community, and the rents are usually reasonable.

"Just work hard and keep an eye on every aspect of the business, including the bookkeeping."

Matthew Carone: Gallery Owner

Matthew Carone is the owner of the Carone Gallery, a prestigious establishment in Fort Lauderdale, Florida. He handles mainly contemporary art—American, some European, and some Latin American paintings and sculpture. He is also an established painter himself and often is invited to show his work at other galleries.

The Carone Gallery, a family business, has been in existence since 1957. "I am the owner, and my wife is my partner," Matthew explains. "My son had been an assistant director, but recently left to work for our symphony here. Now I'm semiretired. I spend five months of the year in Lenox, Massachusetts, in the Tanglewood area where I have a studio, the rest of the time in Fort Lauderdale.

"South Florida's busy season is during the winter months. I've found over the years that during the summer months, if you're lucky, you just make ends meet, so we decided many years ago not to worry about the summers, to just relax, and when people are back in the momentum of buying, we open our doors and everyone is clamoring to come in and see what's new for the year. So we close for five or six months of the year and that works out well.

"I acquire artwork in a couple of ways. I'm now in a position that there are a number of artists who would like to show with me, so I can be very selective. After you have a track record and you've established yourself, you get to that plateau where the artist knows of your reputation and wants to be in your stable of artists, so to speak.

"But when you're starting, you have to trust your taste and look for talent that may yet to be discovered. Establish yourself as a serious gallery. I happened to do it by way of master graphics. I got involved with original prints, not reproductions, but very serious Picassos, very serious Cezanne and Matisse prints, and I got a reputation for that in the early years. This made it easier for me to then work one-on-one with important artists because they knew of my seriousness."

Starting Your Own Gallery

"First you decide what you want to sell and promote," Matthew says. "Being idealistic about it is one way to go, if you have faith in a particular artist but you know his work would be difficult to sell. Great art is not always palatable on your initial response. Even Picasso, before he became famous, was laughed at by most of the people in the world. You have to be brave and have a conviction about the art, and that, of course, comes out of a love for it. You have to be sincere.

"Rental of the space is the main factor," he continues. "I would always look for a space in the best location, even though it might be more expensive. If you can be in a cultural area, near a museum, that would be ideal. To look for a very inexpensive space off the beaten track is not the way to go.

"Think of the cost of a year's rent. Other expenses are minimal. You have blank walls painted white, track lighting, a desk, and a little storeroom. There are advertising costs, brochures, announcements, your insurance and utilities, and any salaries you'll have to pay. That's the beginning.

"Then you have to get a stable of artists who would reflect your taste, who would help establish your image as a serious gallery.

"In a craft gallery it might be easier to sell your inventory, but I wouldn't advise it as a way to get into serious art. If you get established as having a craft gallery, that's almost like a stigma. You always carry that on your back. But it could be financially successful; people love crafts. Success on that level is easier than going for fine arts. More people will respond to a pot than a painting. You'll have a bigger audience.

"The tragedy of the arts is that it caters to only 3 percent of the population. Now that could be quite a bit, if you're in a cultural area, but that 3 percent is distributed among the arts in general—music and arts—so if you want to hone in on just a segment of that, on just painting or just sculpture, there's not that much out there. You're in a minority arena. It's a risky business. But when something happens to have a magic combination, it's good and the public responds to it, that's paradise."

The Day-to-Day Running of an Art Gallery

"During a typical good day during the season—January, February, and March—I come in and put the coffee on, take a look at my show, and then, shortly thereafter, a client comes in and it becomes a social hour," Michael explains. "We sit down and have a cup of coffee and she wants to see what we're showing. We get into dialogue and we're getting excited to the point where she says 'I have to own it.' Or maybe not, or maybe something else. And that happens throughout the day.

"In addition to client contact, I talk with artists, artists who want to show with me. They send me slides, they want to see me, and I never refuse to talk to them. Part of the fun is looking at all the art and deciding who you want to show. The artist might be wonderful with beautiful art, but then you also have to evaluate whether or not you'll be able to sell it. Each space on the wall costs you x amount of money. You have to make your expenses, and every inch of wall space must try to pay for itself.

"You might also talk to the artist you're currently showing. Maybe for some reason his work isn't selling and then you have to console him.

"You also have to concern yourself with the installation of a particular show and where a painting belongs in relation to another painting. Hanging the art is something you need to have a feel for. For instance, I have 10,000 square feet, 5,000 feet on each level, so we have a big, expansive space to hang many different kinds of art. And it's very important to be able to hang an artist next to someone he's compatible with. You don't want any conflicts in image. You wouldn't want to put an ethereal kind of painting next to a very guttural abstract. You could destroy that very sensitive painting if it's within the view of something incompatible. You learn this on the job and through discussion, and it's a gut feeling. There's no one book that can describe this. There is a sense that one feels.

"While you have a show up, you're always anticipating and planning for the next show. I usually do a show for three weeks, then give myself a week off between shows. I don't usually do more than four shows a season. Then, after the shows, you bring out your own inventory, things you own outright that you have accumulated over the years.

"It's been the most wonderful life for me," Michael states. "I can't tell you how great it's been. First of all, I'm a painter, I play the violin, and I use my gallery for concerts. I come to work thinking I'm coming home. I'm going to where I want to be. I love the artists, I love selling important stuff, I love people responding to my enthusiasm. It's been glorious. I'm a very lucky guy—I love what I do."

The Finances Involved

Most galleries work on a 50-50 percentage basis with the artist. "But if it's a very popular artist," Matthew explains, "you might get only 30 percent. The cost of the artwork could range from $2,000 for a small wooden mask to $9,500 for paintings for the show I'm doing now. I've sold art for $43,000, and that's not the most expensive I've shown. With an artist who has a following, the more popular they are, the bigger the attraction they are, the better for you."

Food for Thought

The ideal enterprise for many self-starters is to open a restaurant, café, coffee bar, or some other type of dining establishment. It's a risky business, anyone will tell you, and the trick is to find something new, a twist that will capture the attention of a large audience.

Just as coffee bars in New York City are the popular endeavor now, twenty years ago it was ice cream. Two decades ago, the first Steve's Ice Cream was a groundbreaker in a movement that brought people back to a more natural way of enjoying ice cream. Its founder, self-starter Steve Herrell, wanted to start a fun business, and he thought ice cream would be just the thing.

How Steve Got Started

"Ice cream has been around commercially for 140 years or so," says Steve, "and in the old days it was very good. But it started declining in quality. Around 1973 it had gotten about as low as it could get. At that time there seemed to be a sudden revelation that ice cream could be a lot better than what we'd been getting. There was a whole movement to go back to the basics then, in food and other areas. That's when natural food stores started, vegetarian restaurants, granola—the timing was right.

"I remembered our days at home when I was growing up, making ice cream in the backyard with the family. My dad and my great-uncle taught us all how to make it. We learned about the fun of everyone taking a turn at the crank, and the anticipation when putting in the ice and salt, and the great moment when it was done and opening it up and taking out the dasher.

"I'm a certified high school English teacher in Massachusetts. I had done a little of that but found it was not my cup of tea. I drove a taxi for a couple of years while trying to figure out what I would do with the remainder of my life. I knew it would not be taxi driving. The main thing I knew I wanted to do was run my own business and be in charge. And it was somewhat of a secondary question just what that business might be."

Steve opened up Steve's Ice Cream on Elm Street in Somerville, Massachusetts, on a Friday in June 1973. Within the first three days, he had a full crowd every night. He spent about $200 to advertise on WBCN, a popular radio station in Boston, but it was word of mouth that packed the place. The local press paid Steve's a lot of attention, and articles started appearing regularly in the *Boston Globe*. Not too much later came national recognition. *The New Yorker* was the first; it showcased Steve's Ice Cream in the "Talk of the Town" section.

Steve's was the first parlor to make its own ice cream in full view of all the customers. Steve was also the first to popularize using "Mix-ins," which is now a trademark for the crushed up Heath bars, Oreo cookies, M&Ms and all those other goodies you can blend with your ice cream. Today, it is commonplace, but then it was pure novelty.

"I thought it would be a fun business," Steve explains, "an interesting thing to watch, making ice cream in full view on the premises. What this was was a business concept. I wanted it to be an active kind of a place, a place of function where something would be going on. We had a player piano, colorful pictures on the walls; there was a certain personal atmosphere to the place.

"I earned a BA in sociology; I think, though, that if I had gone to business school and earned a business degree, I would not have done Steve's. Part of its attraction and charm was due to my obvious lack of business training. I was not following any kind of mold—it was a pure vision of what I thought it could be and how it should operate. If I had gone to business school, I might have been taught it wouldn't work."

The Finances Involved

"I started with almost nothing," Steve note. "I used what personal savings I had and credit cards. It wasn't nearly enough, but because of that it was a very personal kind of place. For example, the chairs and tables didn't match. Normally, when opening a restaurant, you'd go out and buy 12 tables and chairs that were all the same. But I went to used furniture stores and picked out two chairs here, three there, and painted them (orange, red, and purple). You wouldn't learn that in a business course.

"And, also, there were generally no books then on how to make ice cream with an ice-and-salt freezer. In fact, the freezer I bought to use there went too fast. The motor moved the dasher too rapidly, and it didn't mimic the action of a hand crank the way I thought it would. But it was a little late at that point, I was due to open in three days. It was pure panic. I took the motor off and put on a gear reducer, which essentially slowed the whole thing down.

"We sold out almost every night. I opened with just one or two employees, and I was making all of the ice cream and staying up every night to do it. I was very happy that it was so successful and so well received right away, but then I had to close for about two weeks to reorganize, to move in more equipment and hire more staff and train them to make ice cream. When I first opened, I didn't even have enough refrigeration space."

Usually with a new business you can't expect to break even or show a profit the first year or so, but that wasn't the case with Steve's. "I always had enough to live on, and there was always a high volume of customers," he says. "The problem with Steve's was that the prices weren't high enough, so it always seemed like there wasn't enough money. So I raised the prices and worried that the customers wouldn't want to come, but there was never any negative feedback. All through my four years there my prices could have been, should have been, at least twenty-five percent higher than they were."

The Formula for Success

Steve attributes his success to a variety of reasons: "I never advertised that the ice cream was all natural, but people just picked that up and assumed it. My hope was to take cream and eggs and sugar and mix it up, flavor it, and freeze it. But health codes don't allow you to do just that in a retail situation. You need to use a prepackaged mixture made by a dairy processor under controlled conditions. The mixture's main ingredients are cream and sugar, and it's homogenized and pasteurized—the pasteurization is an important part of the process. It also has stabilizers to prevent ice crystals from forming during temperature fluctuation and to give the ice cream body and not let it melt too fast. It doesn't have preservatives to make it last longer like you'd find in bread, for example, but it does have additives. The air content in my ice cream is very low, though, which means it tastes richer and you get more substance per teaspoon than in a high air content ice cream.

"Basically, the ice cream tastes great. I do my own flavoring, and that's all natural. I don't go for weird, I go for good. The flavors are unique, such as root beer or Earl Grey tea. Then there's malted vanilla, pure vanilla, pure chocolate, real strawberries in the strawberry.

"The idea of making the ice cream on the premises was unique, the Mix-ins and the store itself all contributed to the success. There was a real character to it. It wasn't a big impersonal chain then, and people could sense that there was a real person behind the whole thing. People related to that and liked it."

After Steve's

"I sold Steve's in August of '77, all assets and liabilities," the entrepreneur explains. "There was a nice difference between my initial investment and the final sale price. The only thing I kept was the player piano. Two brothers and a third partner bought Steve's and expanded it a bit before selling it to a company called Integrated Resources, which then sold it to another partnership. I have no involvement with any of the Steve's you see around the country. The ice cream at Steve's is very different now, and it's not made on-site anymore. The original character has been diluted, which is what tends to happen with a chain.

"I had a three-year noncompetition agreement with the people I sold to. It expired in August of 1980. In September of '80, I opened Herrell's Ice Cream in Northampton, about 90 miles west of Boston, where Mount Holyoke and Smith Colleges are.

"Very soon after that I became interested in expanding and enlisted the services of a franchise consultant. I then opened the first Herrell's franchise store in Harvard Square on Dunster Street in '82. It's still there, and they use all my formulas and trademarks. At this time, there are two other franchises in Boston, as well as an ice cream bon bon plant.

"But Herrell's has a very nonchain feel to it," Steve says. "I used that old player piano for awhile at Herrell's, but these days it's sitting in storage. The customers would play the same songs over and over—"Rubber Ducky" (a favorite of the Smithies), "Maple Leaf Rag," *William Tell* Overture, "The Entertainer Rag"—and drive the staff crazy.

"We have about 1,200 square feet, decorated with Caribbean colors—greens and reds—a tin ceiling, and two giant stuffed bears sitting in the window having a dish of vanilla ice cream."

Steve has 25 employees, and he puts in about 35 hours a week at Herrell's. He's at the point where he could let employees handle the day-to-day tasks, but he prefers to still keep his hand in. "I could be semiretired now, but then I would start to lose touch with what's going on; you don't hear feedback from customers and everything would be secondhand. I always appreciate when a customer comes up and tells me how much they enjoy Herrell's, and lots of people come up to me who remember going to the Somerville store 20 years ago, standing in line, and having that unique ice cream experience."

Some Words of Advice

Steve says you should just go ahead and follow your vision—and don't go to business school. "I would have been more fearful if I had known what problems might have come up. If you get too much advice you could be overwhelmed. I could make a list of all the potential problems and publish it, but it wouldn't be a good idea. Your creativity would get squelched."

To learn more about a different kind of restaurant success story, turn to Chapter Six.

CHAPTER THREE

Service Industry Careers

The service industry leads all others as the largest employer in the United States. It also offers the largest variety of opportunities for self-employed self-starters.

Because it is such a wide-open occupational category, it would be impossible to name all the possibilities. A few key businesses are covered in this chapter. Other types of service endeavors appear in various chapters throughout the book.

How to Choose Your Service

Perhaps you know you want to enter into some sort of service enterprise, but you're not sure of the working conditions the different fields offer or which area would best suit your personality, skills, and lifestyle. There are several factors to consider when deciding which sector of the service industry to pursue. Each field carries with it different levels of responsibility and commitment. To identify occupations that will match your expectations, you need to know what the different services entail.

To help narrow the field, ask yourself the following questions:

- How much of a "people person" are you? Do you prefer to work face to face with clients or customers, or are you more comfortable with telephone contact?
- Do you want a desk job, or would you prefer to be out and about?

- How much time are you willing to commit to training? Some skills can be learned on the job or in a year or two of formal training; others can take considerably longer.
- How much money do you expect to earn after you graduate and after you have a few years' experience under your belt? Salaries and earnings vary greatly in each service profession.

Knowing what your expectations are, then comparing them to the realities of the work, will help you make informed choices.

Personal Services

Beauty and physical fitness have been a concern for a large portion of the population over the last three decades or so. Acquiring the right look has never been easy. It requires that perfect hairstyle, exquisite nails, a neatly trimmed beard or just the right makeup, as well as the best, fine-tuned body you can drum into shape.

Owning your own beauty salon or having your own freelance business is a route many self-starters follow.

Hairstylists and Cosmetologists

As people increasingly demand styles that are better suited to their individual characteristics, they rely on hairstylists and cosmetologists more and more. Although tastes and fashions change from year to year, the basic duties remain the same—to help people look their best.

Hairstylists/cosmetologists primarily shampoo, cut, and style hair. They also may advise patrons on how to care for their own hair. Frequently, they straighten or permanent wave a customer's hair to keep the style in shape. Cosmetologists may also lighten or darken hair color.

In addition, most cosmetologists are trained to give manicures and scalp and facial treatments, provide makeup analysis for women, and clean and style wigs and hairpieces.

Many shop-owning hairstylists still work with clients in addition to their responsibilities for the day-to-day operation of their shop.

Training

Although all states require stylists and cosmetologists to be licensed, the qualifications necessary to obtain a license vary. Generally, a person must have graduated from a state-licensed barber or cosmetology school, pass a physical examination, and be at least 16 years old. In addition, education requirements vary from state to state—some require graduation from high school, whereas others require only an eighth-grade education. In a few states, completion of an apprenticeship can substitute for formal education, but very few stylists or cosmetologists learn their skills in this way. Applicants for a license usually are required to pass a written test and demonstrate an ability to perform basic barbering or cosmetology services.

Some states have reciprocity agreements that allow licensed stylists and cosmetologists to practice in a different state without additional formal training. Other states do not recognize training or licenses obtained elsewhere; consequently, persons who wish to become stylists or cosmetologists should review the laws of the state in which they want to work before entering a training program.

Public and private vocational schools offer day or evening classes in barbering and cosmetology. These programs usually last six to twelve months. An apprenticeship program can last from one to two years.

Formal training programs include classroom study, demonstrations, and practical work. Students study the basic services of haircutting, shaving, facial massage, and hair and scalp treatments and, under supervision, practice on customers in school clinics. Most schools also teach unisex hairstyling and chemical styling. Students attend lectures on barber services, the use and care of instruments, sanitation and hygiene, and recognition of certain skin ailments.

Instruction also is given in selling and general business practices. There are advanced courses for experienced barbers in hairstyling, coloring, and the sale and service of hairpieces. Most schools teach styling of both men's and women's hair.

After graduating from a training program, students can take the state licensing examination. The examination consists of a written test and, in some cases, a practical test of cosmetology skills. A few states include an oral examination in which the applicant is asked to explain the procedures he or she is following while taking the practical test. In some states, a separate examination is given for persons who want only a manicurist or facial care license.

Many schools help their graduates find employment. During their first months on the job, new workers are given relatively simple tasks, such as giving shampoos, or are assigned to perform the simpler hairstyling patterns. Once they have demonstrated their skills, they are gradually permitted to perform the more complicated tasks such as giving shaves, coloring hair, or applying permanents.

Michael Silvestri: Hairstylist

Michael Silvestri has been in the business for over 30 years, both as a salaried hairstylist and as the owner of his own salons.

"It's great, it's really interesting work," says Michael. "I love people. If you didn't, you couldn't stay in this business. Today, most of my best friends are people I've met in the industry, mostly clients.

"The downside of it for me, as a shop owner, was that I never had as much difficulty with clients as I did with other hairstylists. As a coworker that was easy, but when I was the boss, the hairdressers were very difficult. They're a different breed—their mind-set. I don't know if it was the artistic temperament or what, but so many different things entered into it. For a long time there was a huge drug-abuse problem. You'd find out that one of your top stylists was a drug user, then what were you going to do about it?

"If you let people go, you're going to lose business. When your hairstylists move on to another salon they take their clients with them, and there's nothing you can do about that. As an owner, this is always first on your mind. You have to kow tow to very tempera-mental people and sometimes unreliable people. They wouldn't show up to work or they'd be late, but you couldn't afford to fire them.

"This is one of the reasons I choose not to be an owner anymore. For most of my career I have been an owner, and though I liked it enough to stay with it that long, as an independent hairstylist I have a lot more freedom. For example, I just took a vacation. I hadn't had a vacation in nine years. As an owner, you have to always be there, you have to watch what's going on, you have to watch the register, otherwise you won't make any money. It's largely a cash business. They can take what they want from you and you wouldn't know."

The Finances Involved

"The advantage, of course, to being an owner is that you have the opportunity to make a lot more money," Michael states. "If it all clicks, you've got it good. When I had the two salons going and we had 26 employees, we were doing very well. And, of course, there's the satisfaction when you do well—starting a business and watching it grow.

"But it fluctuates. There's less security. Because the employees come and go, you could go from 26 employees down to 15, but you have the same overhead. The hours are terrible, and you need a huge financial outlay to start a business. You'd probably need at least $75,000 now to do it.

"When you're not an owner, you can pick and choose where you're going to work, set your own hours. If you don't want to work six hours, you can work four. It's up to you.

"How much money you make depends on how good you are. It also depends on the type of salon you work in. The upscale ones that charge more money for their services are going to generally pay you more. You'd make any combination of a salary, plus commission, plus tips. Commissions can run from 40 to 70 percent. Base salary could be as low as a couple of hundred a week. Just something to get you started. Tips would fluctuate wildly. A shampoo assistant might earn $40 or $50 a week; a hair dresser could pull in as much as $300 or $400 a week."

What the Work Is Really Like

"In dealing with clients, you have to spend time with them, learn about them, and help them get over any past bad experiences they've had at the hairdressers," notes Michael. "You might decide what you believe will look good on them, but then you have to be able to convince them that it will work. Sometimes it takes more than one appointment to get comfortable with each other. But one mistake, you could lose that client forever.

"It's very hard work, very tiring work. Most people don't understand that, but you're on your feet all day. Hairdressers wind up with bad backs, or bad necks, or some kind of foot problem. Carpal tunnel syndrome goes with it, too. And I'm allergic to a lot of the products we use, the mousses and gels. My skin will break out, and you can't really wear gloves.

"But I love to work with clients, especially new ones. It's great to take someone and make her over, make her look totally different than when she came in. That's the fun part."

How Michael Got Started

"I was influenced by family members," he explains. "My uncle was a men's barber. At the time, I was on Wall Street working as a stock transfer clerk and not very happy. I didn't like the office atmosphere. My uncle would hear me complain when I came home at night and he suggested I go to school. The first thing I thought was why would I want to do that. I had no idea that I had an inclination to do that sort of thing. He kept pushing it and after a while he wore me down and I decided to try it.

"So, when I was 17, within seven months after graduating high school I enrolled in hairdressing school. The program was about a year, and I studied at a private academy. That was 1961.

"After I finished, I apprenticed myself. At that time, the only way a male hairdresser could get a job was to sign into servitude. I got a couple of jobs in the area as a shampooer, but worked for free for about nine months. But I really learned, and I also got a few tips here and there. I also took a month's course at Charles of the Ritz in New York, which at the time was considered a very good hairstyling academy.

"Then, I was finally hired on as a hairdresser at one of the shops I had apprenticed in. That was the start of my career. I worked in a variety of shops, then in 1965 I opened my first shop. I did that for six years, then in 1973 I relocated to the south.

"I went to work for a real top-flight guy I had met in Philadelphia and stayed with him for about two years. One of his employees left him to open his own shop and invited me along. I was his operator/ manager for about ten years.

"In 1984 I opened my own shop with a partner and in 1990 we opened another salon. But I wasn't very happy, so in 1994 I sold both shops and went to work as an employee in another salon. And that's what I'm doing now."

Pitfalls to Avoid

"I used to always give my new employees a talk before they got started," Michael recalls. "I'd say, 'Remember that the first time you get a new client, she's probably scared to death. She doesn't know you, she doesn't know your place. You've got a strange instrument in your hand—a pair of scissors—and that can cause some serious damage. People do some crazy things with haircuts. So, it's up to you to make her comfortable.' A lot of hairdressers don't bother to do that, but I think it's very important for a new client. You have to spend time consulting with them, taking their lifestyle into consideration, the shape of their face, and what kind of hair they have. Then you can go to work, but not before.

"And if you're going into this business, you have to have an independent streak in you, you can't be afraid. You're going to function as an independent contractor for your whole career, so you have to be able to take care of yourself.

"Then you have to decide that you're willing to work hard enough to make this work. If you're lazy, you won't make any money. It will take a while to build up a clientele, as well as your skills and confidence. You have to be prepared for one or two lean years."

Robin Landry: Esthetician

Whereas a cosmetologist is trained primarily in hair care, an esthetician works exclusively with skin care. Robin Landry is a skin-care professional working freelance as an independent contractor.

"It doesn't look as if I work for myself because I operate out of two different salons," she explains, "but in actuality, I do. I'm paid on commission. The salons give me a workplace—I don't have to pay rent or other overhead expenses—they provide me with all my products and supplies, and for that they take a 35-percent cut. I also get tips and a percentage—an average of 15 percent—on the beauty products I sell to my clients.

"In addition, being on the premises provides me with a captive audience, so to speak. But, of course, once they put the clients into my hands, it's up to me to make sure they keep coming back.

"It's a great feeling to, first of all, make someone feel good. And also to see the results of your work on something as personal as someone's skin. That's very, very personal, and I think it takes a little bit of a push to get someone to admit they need help with that, but once they do, they look up to me as someone who *can* help them. And sometimes I'm simply amazed at the results I get.

"To keep your clients happy requires professionalism. A lot of people can give a good facial, but a good bedside manner and my professionalism really make a big difference. And I keep them coming back with a good product. I believe in what I sell and in what I do. That says a lot to my clients."

Behind the Scenes

"Giving the actual facial is a very relaxing hour and fifteen minutes, for both my clients and myself," Robin acknowledges. "Clients do remark on that. They're very envious of my silent, quiet job. But they only see that side of it. They don't see the frustrations.

"I work only four days a week. But one of my days is a 12-hour day, another is nine hours, and the other two are 8 hours. I give myself three days off because you can get very burnt out in this business. The clients drain you of everything you can possibly give.

You have at least 20 questions coming out of each client's mouth; they each have their own stories and beliefs on products and ingredients in products. So you really have to stand strong and be knowledgeable. You're always having to defend your position.

"Not only do you have to keep up with your schedule, which can be back to back and very hectic, in the interim you have to sell products, and you have to keep a file on each client. This helps you keep track of which treatments you've done on them, which products you've sold to them. And selling the products is very important. Retail is where you make your money.

"Another frustration is with appointments. People don't show up. I've tried to incorporate a policy that they will be billed 50 percent if they don't give 24 hours notice. I've probably had only one person pay, though. In the end, I don't really enforce it.

"Another difficult aspect is that your performance and your appearance always have to be a '10.' That can be tricky, keeping yourself together when you're running like a crazy person all day. Your hair falls out of its scrunchy, and your lipstick wears off, and it's four hours before you have time to put more on. I always make sure to do that, though. I wear a cake powder so my skin always looks good, and I make sure I always have lipstick on.

"But it feels good, being your own boss, and being in charge of your own success."

The Finances Involved

"A facial costs about $50, waxing ranges from $8 to $45, and makeup can cost from $25 to $55—but on top of that, some clients might leave with $150 worth of products," notes Robin. "But you have to have the product in stock, or else you'll lose the sale. The salon shelves should be stocked with these products, but you end up hearing all these sob stories from the owners—when they can order, how much they can afford to order. I do the actual ordering, I take on that responsibility to make sure the orders get in to the representatives, but first I have to clear it through the owners."

How Robin Got Started

"I was going to school for massage therapy to begin with," she re-members. "But a month or two into the program I fell and broke my wrist. I was out of work and in occupational therapy for two years with that wrist. There were major complications. Finally, I was able to work and I had jobs with a chiropractor and a dentist. I was really involved with one-on-one patient care a lot. I always liked that. But, I did not appreciate not being appreciated. By my employers, that is, not the patients. So I had to decide to do something for myself, with myself, by myself, and be able to thank myself for it. I decided to go back to school, this time for skin care. And that was only because there was some massage involved in it and I was more impressed with that than any of the other areas of the esthetic industry.

"I went to a private career institute and studied formally for six months. My areas are mainly skin care, makeup, and waxing. When I finished the program, I took the test and got my license. Since then, over the past three years, I've had ongoing training with continuing education courses and seminars through the product manufacturers."

Some Tips from Robin

"I would highly recommend a career in skin care. I consider it more glamorous and less taxing than working with hair and nails," she advises.

"And I think you're better off working on a percentage basis than renting the space yourself. I did that the first year and lost some money. You can make a good living, but it's unpredictable. You never know how much you're going to earn. You need to give yourself time to gradually and consistently build up your business.

"Above all else, you have to keep yourself knowledgeable about your work and your products. People will believe in you if you show them that you're confident in what you're doing."

Personal Trainers

Personal trainers work in health clubs, spas, and gyms or in private practice. Their work is, in many ways, similar to that of the physical therapist, although personal trainers tend to work with a more well, albeit out-of-shape, population.

Training

To meet safety standards and insurance, state, and local regulations, most health club–type settings require their instructors and trainers to have appropriate qualifications or licenses. Personal trainers hold a great deal of responsibility for their clients' welfare and must be fully trained in what they do.

There are a few routes trainers can take to learn their craft and become certified. Some universities offer exercise science or exercise physiology programs. You can also do home study through the American Council on Exercise (ACE), then sit for the exam they give twice a year. The American College of Sports Medicine (ACSM) is also a certifying body.

Both organizations' tests have written and practical components. The practical test consists of sub-max testing where you are evaluated while you monitor a client's heart rate and blood pressure. You also put your client through a workout, and your spotting techniques and interaction with the client will be judged.

A training program can take two weeks, eight weeks, or four years, if you pursue a bachelor's degree. Once you have become a personal trainer you'll need continuing education credits to keep up your certification.

Frank Cassisa: Certified Personal Trainer

Frank Cassisa is a certified personal trainer at a national health and fitness chain. He works as an independent contractor.

"Fitness instruction is just like computers; it's always changing, there's always something new coming out. To be the best trainer, you have to stay on top of everything.

"One of the best settings is working in a health club," explains Frank." You don't have to generate business because the business is already there in the club. You can also have a private practice, at your own place or going to people's home. But once you're outside of a club setting, you're talking totally different insurance coverage. If you work out of your own home or in a client's home, you need to cover yourself. You're more open for a lawsuit, God forbid something happened to the client. At a club, you come under their insurance.

"I work for a club and I'm covered by their insurance, but even then it doesn't mean someone couldn't come after me personally. But it would have to be plain stupidity to do something that could cause a client to get hurt. Safety is the key."

"We have to check the equipment before the client actually uses it. You have to be fully aware of the human body and how it should move and shouldn't move. If there are any complications or special populations you're working with—diabetics, for example, or rehab cardiac patients, people with arthritis, or pregnant women—there are different ways to train them."

"When you're a certified personal trainer you're not only learning about nutrition and kinesiology, which is the study of the movement of the body, learning how the muscles react to certain exercises, you also learn first aid. All certified personal trainers must be certified in CPR."

"With the general population," he continues, "people who want to improve their fitness, you first have to take a health history, get their doctor's name and number, and ask the right questions—age, smoking, any history of health risk factors. If we feel this person is not ready for a training program, we'll tell them 'no' and have them contact their doctor for a physical."

"The perfect scenario for someone not ready is the 45-year-old male who smokes, is overweight, and somebody in his family had diabetes. This person could be a walking time bomb. It would be up to the doctor to do a stress test and see if he's ready. We don't do any diagnosing; we can only suspect. We're not doctors or dietitians; we have to refer clients to professionals if we feel we can't answer their questions or their condition needs medical attention."

"If a client is a go-ahead, we assess him or her and try to get in all the elements of physical fitness, such as flexibility, muscular strength and endurance, cardiovascular endurance, and body composition. Normally a training session is an hour. Clients come once or twice a week to meet with the trainer. And they should come on their own the other days."

How Frank Got Started

"For me it's always been my hobby, but now I'm getting paid for it," he recalls. "I studied through ACE and took their two-part exam, a written and a practical. I love to work out and I love to teach people. I work five days a week. When I take my two-hour lunch break, I'm working out. You have to be driven and absorb the whole lifestyle."

The Finances Involved

Personal trainers in a health club can work on commission or an hourly rate, earning anywhere from $45 to $150 an hour, depending on the budget of the clientele.

They can set their own hours, train four people in a day and be done, if they choose. But if self-employed, personal trainers have taxes and insurance expenses, too.

Expert Advice from Frank

"You need a great attitude and you have to practice what you preach. To a client you're a friend, father figure, role model. They'll follow someone who has the results they're looking for.

"Caring is also important," he notes. "You need a firm hand but diplomatic skills. You're an instructor, not a dictator."

Other Services

As mentioned earlier, in addition to personal services, there is a wide spectrum of service careers to pursue as an independent contractor or your own boss. Further exploration or brainstorming on your part will reveal more possibilities.

What follows are just three examples of interesting and unusual self-starter service enterprises.

Auctioneers

"I have this nice oak roll top desk, how about a five hundred dollar bid, get five hundred, get five hundred, get two and a half, start us off, give us a hundred, give a hundred . . .," is part of the chant you'll hear from auctioneer Jim Ridolfi, owner of the Aspon Trading Company in Troy, Pennsylvania.

"Everyone has a chant, and everyone develops their own. I try not to use too many words—the people won't understand you. What they're listening for is the numbers. You learn a basic method at auctioneer training school, and then you take it and refine it and make it into your own."

Training for Auctioneers

Training programs can run from two weeks to three or four months, depending on your state's requirements. Different states have different licensing laws. Some states have none at all; some are very rigorous with what they require. While in training, auctioneers also study communication skills, the law as it applies to auctioneers, marketing and advertising, auction management, appraisal, and real estate.

Many auctioneers go through various national auctioneering schools; the best-known one is the Missouri Auction School. But it's important to check first which schools your state will accept.

Pennsylvania, for example, only accepts training through the two schools in Pennsylvania. The best thing to do is contact your state licensing board and find out what it requires, then write or call The National Auctioneers Association (listed in Appendix A) to find the appropriate training.

How Jim Got Started

Like Jim Ridolfi, many auctioneers are also antique dealers. Jim specializes in old phonographs and radios and has a particular love for mid– to late–nineteenth-century items. In addition to antiques, auctioneers also handle household items, livestock, and real estate.

Jim became an auctioneer in 1992. He advertises his services in newspapers and has made contacts with other antique dealers, estate attorneys, and will executors.

The Finances Involved

Auctioneers hold their events indoors in hotel ballrooms or outside in a farmer's field or an estate's backyard. Some locations are provided rent-free, whereas with others there may be a charge.

Auctioneers work on a percentage basis, earning between 15 and 30 percent of the price of each item sold.

Related Work in the Field

In addition to your future role as an auctioneer, you might find yourself supervising other employees, such as these:

- Runners move the items for sale from the holding area to the stage.
- Floor managers supervise the runners, let them know which items are going up next, and take care of any other details so the auctioneer is not distracted.
- Clerks make a record of the proceedings and handle the numbering of lots and bidders.
- Cashiers collect the money.

- Security guards watch over the sold items while they're waiting to be picked up.
- Caterers provide the refreshments for the audience and staff.
- Advertisers/marketers help the auctioneer inform the public about his or her services and particular auction events.
- Catalogers work with large estates, organizing the items and taking precise inventories.
- Appraisers help authenticate and place a value on particular items.
- Furniture refinishers and restorers, although not usually directly involved with an auction, find work with dealers or private individuals giving life back to old or damaged items.
- Flea market/antique show organizers put on the big events that attract thousands of people. They handle every detail, including advertising, allocating space, and collecting fees.

Genealogists

The study of genealogy, tracing family histories, has recently become one of the most popular hobbies in the United States. Almost everyone has a keen interest in their family background. Many hobbyists take their interest one step further and become self-employed genealogists, helping others dig up their family trees. Genealogists also are employed in historical societies and libraries with special genealogy rooms. The Church of Jesus Christ of Latter Day Saints in Salt Lake City, for example, has a huge repository of family information in a subterranean library. The church employs genealogists all over the world or includes genealogists who have been accredited through its own program on a list of freelance researchers. For more information, write or call the library at the listing in Appendix A.

Other genealogists find work teaching their skills to others in adult education classes, editing genealogy magazines, or writing books or newspaper genealogy columns.

Most genealogists are not formally trained, although it is possible to specialize in genealogy through some university history and library science programs. In addition, a genealogist can become board certified. Information on certification requirements and procedures may be obtained from the Board for Certification of Genealogists, listed in Appendix A.

Salaries

Salaries vary depending on the institution where a genealogist is employed and on the level of expertise he or she has reached. Self-employed genealogists make anywhere from $15 to $35 an hour.

How to Get Started

The National Genealogy Society makes the following suggestions for beginners:

1. Question older family members. Encourage them to talk about their childhoods and relatives, and listen carefully for clues they might inadvertently drop. Learn good interviewing techniques so you ask questions that elicit the most productive answers. Use a tape recorder and try to verify each fact through a separate source.

2. Visit your local library. Become familiar with historical and gene-alogical publications (a few sources are provided in Appendix A), and contact local historical societies and the state library and archives in your state capital. Seek out any special ethnic or religious libraries, and visit cemeteries.

3. Visit courthouses. Cultivate friendships with busy court clerks. Ask to see source records, such as wills, deeds, marriage books, and birth and death certificates.

4. Enter into correspondence. Write to other individuals or soci-eties involved with the same families or regions. Contact foreign embassies in Washington, DC. Restrict yourself to asking only one question in each letter you send. Include the information you

have already uncovered, and enclose a self-addressed stamped envelope to encourage replies.

5. Become computer literate. Members of the National Genealogical Society can participate in a special computer-interest section. It encourages the use of computers in research, record management, and data sharing.

6. Keep painstaking records. Use printed family group sheets or pedigree charts. Develop a well-organized filing system so you'll be able to easily find your information. Keep separate records for each family you research.

7. Write the National Genealogical Society. Take advantage of the society's 46-page book, *Beginners in Genealogy*, its charts, and its library loan program. You can also enroll in its home-study course called "American Genealogy: A Basic Course."

Tree Trimming

Way Hoyt is owner of Tree Trimmers and Associates, Inc. "The trees are our associates," Way says. "They have a big part in our business."

Way's wife, Geri, is the owner of Arborist Supply House, which sells ropes, saddles, pruners, shears, and other equipment for tree workers.

Way has been planting trees ever since he was about seven years old. "I'm the little kid who ran along the turnpike taking Australian Pine saplings out, then transplanting them in my yard. I didn't get in trouble with my folks for doing that until the trees grew to be humongous."

Way has an associate's degree and attended the University of Florida at the research and experimental station in Fort Lauderdale. He has been in business more than 18 years.

"I chose self-employment first for financial reasons. Also, when I was working for other companies, I found out that they were basically doing terrible things to the trees. I went into my own business so I could do proper tree trimming.

"Pruning done correctly is the healthiest thing a tree can have done to it. Done incorrectly—as in stubs, nubs, rips, tears, flesh cuts, too much green being removed, or not enough attention paid to structural material—it can be the worst treatment done to the tree."

One of Way's concerns about the profession is the abundance of what he calls hat-rack specialists. "This is a term used for mutilating trees, and that's what an awful lot of tree services continue to do. There are right ways and wrong ways of treating trees and there is a world of information on tree trimming, but it's been my experience that a large percentage of tree trimmers don't know anything about it. Anybody who can work a chain saw thinks he can trim a tree, and anybody can hang out a shingle and call themselves an arborist, even if they're not. All that is required is a small fee to the county for an occupational license and then you can legally call yourself a tree expert."

Way is also concerned about conservation. His company slogan is "a tree company with our environment and associated ecology, performing tree work both scientifically and esthetically."

Way encourages people to attend good programs and get the proper training. He also teaches courses on arboriculture, tree identification, and what happens inside a tree when it's been damaged on the outside.

In addition, he has been asked to appear as an expert witness in court on numerous occasions. He talks about his most recent case: "A fellow was driving east during stormy weather along a four-lane highway with a median strip. The trunk of a black olive tree split and fell on his car as he was driving by at about 45 to 50 miles per hour. He was seriously injured, permanently paralyzed in fact.

"A few months before the accident, the tree had been trimmed. I took a look at the tree and saw indications of serious structural problems. The trimming done was not adequate. They should have notified the property owner of a possible dangerous situation, but they didn't. The professional maintenance company and the condominium complex that own the tree are being sued.

"When I go into court, I'll talk about the tree and the structure and that it was an accident waiting to happen."

Summing up his feelings about his profession, Way says, "You can certainly make a career out of it and never stop learning. And it's very satisfying. You can step back and look at what you have accomplished and know that you did a nice job, helping a tree."

Careers for Performers

*I*s there a bit of the performer in you? Do you definitely not want to be tied to a desk and a 40-hour-a-week commitment? Are you looking for something unusual, something different, to do?

Many innovative people have combined their love of self-employment with other talents or acquired skills. With a good imagination, a dedicated self-starter can bring in extra income or carve out a specialized career. Here are a couple of successful ventures that might spark some ideas of your own.

Walking Tours

If you're comfortable talking with small groups of people, like to walk, know how to conduct research, and can put together a one-to two-hour presentation, then starting a walking tour might be a fun way to start off your self-employment. You won't get rich at first, if ever, but you can probably bring in some additional earnings.

There are different kinds of tours you can organize, depending on how rich in history and local color the place you live is. Here are just a few themes to consider:

Mystery walking tour—highlighting locations of unusual or un-solved crimes or the homes of notorious residents.

Architectural walking tour—featuring homes and buildings of unusual interest. Some examples include the Art Deco District in Miami, the French Quarter in New Orleans, or the stately homes of Charleston, South Carolina.

Literary walking tour—focusing on the homes and lives of famous local writers.

Mystery Walking Tours

Basically, the leader of a mystery walking tour escorts a group of (paying) people to designated sites and landmarks in a particular area. At each stop, the leader gives a talk on that particular spot, telling about its history or notoriety and answering questions.

Mystery walking tours are usually organized around a particular theme. Stops on the route can cover homes of famous mystery writers or may focus on where crimes or scandals occurred. For example, a tour of Boston could follow the killing spree route of the Boston Strangler. Palm Beach, Florida, offers plenty of grist for the gossip mill, and even an island as small as Key West has had its share of titillating incidents.

How far you can go with this idea depends in part on where you live and how active criminals or mystery writers are in your area.

Follow these ten steps to get started:

1. Research your area. Visit the public library, check courthouse records, and ask to be allowed into the newspaper morgue. You're looking for past events or notorious residents, but remember, they must all be within walking distance of each other.

2. If your research is fruitful, decide how long a tour you have material for. Then organize your information to follow the different stops you'll make. Allow ten minutes or so for each spot. Make sure you have as many juicy details as possible. Gory and gruesome work well, too. (Remember, everyone loves a good mystery!)

3. Decide on a price. You probably won't get rich doing this, but don't scare off customers with too high an admission ticket. Anywhere from $4 to $7 is a good ballpark figure to charge each person. You can give discounts for children or senior citizens. The more you have in your group, the more you'll make.

4. How often will you offer the tour? Every Saturday morning? Sunday afternoons? If the area warrants it, you could run one or two a day. It's up to you.

5. Make a dry run. Walk the tour yourself or take along friends and family. It's doubtful that you'll be able to enter any of the buildings without making some sort of arrangement with owners, so be sure to pick out a spot where you and your group can pause to talk. Under a shady tree is good for summer days, but be careful not to block vehicular or pedestrian traffic.

6. Check with local officials regarding any zoning restrictions or occupational licenses or permits you might need.

7. You're now ready to make the leap to tour leader. First, you'll want to stop in at various hotels, visitor centers, chambers of commerce, historical societies, or any other spots that tourists or residents might frequent to see if you'll be able to leave pamphlets on display for prospective customers. Your plan most likely will be met with enthusiasm. These types of establishments are usually glad to help advertise events. Many hotels already keep racks in their lobby filled with pamphlets for various local attractions.

8. You'll need to design and print a brochure that details your tour, how people can contact you, the times and dates you operate, and how much the tour will cost.

9. Find additional ways to promote your tour. Create a press release to send to newspapers; most regularly publish a calendar of events. Contact local radio stations and drop in at bookstores (a favorite hangout for mystery buffs).

10. Buy a pair of good walking shoes (Panama hat is optional), dig out the sunscreen and get ready to have fun.

David Kaufelt's Key West Walking Tour

David Kaufelt is a noted mystery writer and founder of the annual Key West Literary Seminar. While organizing the first year's events, David put together a mystery walking tour of the island to entertain seminar participants. Here's what he has to say about the enterprise: "Key West is the scene of many funny mysteries and murders that have never been solved. I'd been reading about them hither and yon and I'd done some research for an article I wrote on the subject, and from that came the idea to start the Mystery Walking Tour. We needed some money for the Key West Literary Seminar and I thought that this would be a good way to raise some funds. We've always done a tour of great writers' houses in Key West and the mystery tour is an offshoot of that. We do the tours when someone requests them.

"I did some research on the different houses and some of the events I knew because they happened in my time. For example, there was a huge mansion around the corner from where we used to live in Old Town. There was a young man who lived there who no one had seen in quite some time. He'd lived with another man there and they used to fight all the time. As it turned out, the young guy had been an alcoholic and he had died, but the older guy he lived with didn't recognize his death. He thought he was just being ornery. So he'd go get him food every day and told people how he would never speak to him, he was so ornery. But then we all started smelling something strange, and the police were finally notified. The young guy had been dead for months and had almost melted into the linoleum floor in the kitchen. The older man's mind had gone, and his family came and took him away and put him someplace.

"There's another story I like. There's an old boarding house being converted into a hotel over on Simonton Street. It used to be called the Q Rooms and a lot of strange things happened there.

One night a young guy in his twenties was walking home while the building was under construction, and he saw two pairs of legs sticking out. One pair belonged to a woman, and as he looked at the legs he realized he knew her. She was his fiancée, and she was wearing an anklet he had given her. So he pulled her out by the ankles and saw that she was dead. He pulled out the other body, who turned out to be his best friend. The couple had been making love and the "friend" had accidentally killed her. He was alive, but had passed out.

"We also go to the cemetery on the tour; there's always a funny murder there to talk about.

"If you want to start a mystery walking tour, you should do your research very well and be entertaining. You need to be able to tell an anecdote with a punchline.

"But what I would really suggest is that you try to get an organization behind you, such as Mystery Writers of America or Sisters in Crime. You could even try to find an Elder Hostel program in your area and hook up with them. People come to a city to learn and groups organize different events for them.

"You need to be in a good area to do this, Baltimore or Charleston, for example. Make sure you have something with which to identify yourself for people who will be meeting you on a street corner. It could be a T-shirt with a logo printed on it or a banner you can wave.

"And try also to get other people to share in giving the tours. After a while, it can get stale."

Miami Beach's Art Deco District

Jeff Donnelly is a volunteer tour guide for the Miami Design Preservation League. Although he doesn't get paid for his tour, that doesn't mean another enterprising person couldn't start a similar one as a paid guide.

For the past five years on Saturday mornings, Jeff's been donning his Panama hat and walking shoes and taking groups on 90-minute strolling tours through Miami Beach's newly restored Art Deco District. Come join the tour and see how it's done: "Miami Beach is an exciting place to live these days. Young professionals, artists, models, movie production people—they're all flocking here now. We've become very chic," explains Jeff.

After cautioning the 20 or so in his group—from New York, Texas, Colorado, nearby Fort Lauderdale—about the strong Florida sun ("If anyone feels dehydrated, please raise your hand before you pass out"), he provides them with more than just a passing glimpse into Miami's new mystique.

"As elderly residents moved into nursing homes or passed away, investors and developers began buying up and renovating the run-down buildings," he says. "In the process they uncovered the fantasy seaside resort that had first inspired the original boom back in the 1920s and 1930s.

"There were five major architects responsible for the district. Although they were commercial competitors, they were also coffee-klatch friends. If someone's building supplies hadn't arrived on time or if someone ran short, they lent materials back and forth. This, of course, explains the high level of style consistency throughout the district."

The old establishments, once painted white and trimmed with only powder blue, aquamarine, or the peaches and pinks of aging flamingos, have now received fresh face-lifts and glow with a contemporary pastel palette. Bands of lavender, blue, yellow, aqua, and a whole spectrum of pinks whimsically decorate oceanfront hotels, sidewalk cafés, model agencies, and apartment buildings.

Miami Beach can boast of the largest concentration of art deco buildings in the country; over 800 contribute to the historic or architectural nature of the Art Deco District. The result is a Disneyesque urban streetscape, as fanciful as Victorian gingerbread, with the promise of campy humor and fun.

"You'd almost expect to see flappers strolling arm in arm or Al Capone roaring up in his jalopy," observed one member of the tour group.

In fact, it's rumored that Al Capone often ate at the Park Central, one of the hotels along Ocean Drive, his bodyguards perched on the overhead balcony for protection. Whether true or not, the gangster movie *Scarface* was definitely filmed there.

The term *art deco*, a form of art combining art moderne, cubism, futurism and expressionism, wasn't coined until 1968. In its day, Miami Beach's architecture was considered ultramodern; the goal was to be futuristic, to look ahead. In the grip of the Great Depression, the architects and designers wanted to convey the message that happy days were coming.

But the art deco area is not an historic district that seeks to preserve exactly what was there in the twenties and thirties. "We're not a Williamsburg," says Jeff. "Our philosophy is what we call 'adaptive reuse'—restoration projects focus on designs with contemporary uses. It allows for a larger variety of colors and for more of the surface areas to be given over to color."

Anyone who wants to renovate must bring their plans to the Miami Preservation League Review Board for approval. "The Tuesday night meetings are a great source of local entertainment," notes Jeff. "The number of arguments presented over color choices are fascinating."

The Miami Design Preservation League was established in 1976 and is the oldest art deco organization in the world. For three years it cataloged the art deco and Mediterranean revival-style buildings, earning a listing on the National Register of Historic Places. The league's main function now is to guard against demolitions, incompatible construction, and false restorations.

"We don't want new construction to completely imitate the old style," Jeff says. "There's a Kentucky Fried Chicken that slipped by before the review board was established. It looks so much like a building from the twenties, it confuses people."

But the hotels that line Ocean Drive are the real thing. Many are named after posh New York establishments to convey a sense of luxury—the Ritz, the Waldorf Towers; some are named after the designers' family members—the Victor, the Adrian.

And it's not only the bright colors that attract the eye. Special attention to form, detail, and vertical and horizontal lines makes up the art deco style. Buildings have varying themes: streamline moderne rounded corners accented with "eyebrows," sky-pointing needle-like finials (the Breakwater Hotel's allegedly was used in an early Buck Rogers film), rare etched-glass windows, fluted cornices, stepped rooflines, horizontal racing stripes, and nautical moderne porthole windows.

The Avalon Hotel has added a special touch to complete the pretty picture—a 1950 shiny chrome and yellow and white Oldsmobile is regularly parked in front of the yellow-painted building. Quite a number of advertising and model agencies use the hotel for a backdrop for photographic shoots.

Indeed, any morning of the week, when the early eastern light splashes across the soft colors, five or six different shoots are usually in progress. Miami Vice scenes were frequently shot along Ocean Drive, and more and more celebrities visit the area.

Regular special events add even more life to this spirited district. One of these events is the Art Deco Weekend, held annually on the second weekend of January. It relives the days of the Big Band, speakeasies, and street theater against Miami Beach's classic art deco backdrop. Antique cars, period artwork, collectibles, and memorabilia carry visitors back to the Roaring Twenties and thirties.

Nighttime brings a new dimension to the Art Deco District. Neon tube lighting was first invented in the late thirties, and Ocean Drive was a showcase for this exciting new discovery. "It must have been a magical experience for those seeing the glowing colorful lights against the glass block for the first time," says Jeff.

Many of the lobbies inside the hotels are equally magical. Original murals and paintings of the era decorate the walls, and colorful terrazzo stone chips cover the floors in geometric patterns.

Jeff points out the last stop, the Blackstone Hotel, where George Gershwin reputedly wrote *Porgy and Bess*, then steers his group back to the Art Deco Welcome Center.

"It's ironic, really," he concludes. "We've put a lot of effort into preserving an era which actually stood for forward movement, growth, and development. But the architects of the time hit on just the right note for Miami Beach. What was beautiful then is even more beautiful now. It's certainly worth preserving."

For more information on the Art Deco District, the January weekend, or hotel reservations contact Miami Design Preservation League at the address listed in Appendix A.

Murder Mystery Dinners

For the past ten years or so, a new form of entertainment especially designed to appeal to mystery buffs has gained popularity across the country. No longer do restaurant-goers have only their companions and food to keep them occupied. Some enterprising entrepreneurs have arranged for a waiter or waitress, a cook, or perhaps even someone dining at your table to keel over dead in front of your eyes. Shot, stabbed, or maybe even poisoned. Whodunit? That's for diners to figure out.

If you're interested in combining your love of mystery with the drama and glamour of theater, then listen to what producer Connie Gay has to say about murder mystery dinners. She and her husband Jeffrey are producers, directors, and writers for a series of shows they perform under their trademark name, MurderWatch Mystery Theater.

"About eight years ago Jeffrey and I were still living up north in Wakefield, Massachusetts, and doing legitimate theater—musicals such as *Anything Goes, Mame, Hello Dolly*, that sort of thing," Connie explains. "We were involved with community theater and school theater; we did the acting, directing, and producing. We decided we wanted to do a different kind of theater; we were tired of doing the same old thing. So we traveled cross-country to see what was new in theater. What seemed to be pretty popular in all the major cities was mystery shows. They were what I called 'first generation' mystery shows. There would be a murder that would happen backstage. You'd be sitting in a room eating, and if you happened to be at the right table you got the right set of clues, but if you weren't in the right location in the room, you didn't really see much of a show. We weren't really thrilled with the quality of the script of the show, but it was definitely a fun genre, we thought.

"So we discussed it on the plane ride back from our trip and decided to make it a musical mystery show. None of them had music and that would really round out the entertainment end of it. And we wanted to make it so it was more of an environmental theater. The murder would be a theatrical spectacle. It would happen right in the room, and the body would be carried out in front of the guests. We knew that if we handled it with the right amount of humor, it wouldn't be offensive to anyone.

"We've been in the Baskerville's Restaurant at the Grosvenor Resort Hotel in Lake Buena Vista, Florida, for about seven years now. The restaurant has a Sherlock Holmes theme. Every Saturday night guests get to play detective and they also might become suspects. We make sure that there's activity in every section of the room. We make it so everyone sees something, no one sees everything, and everyone gets caught in the act."

How Connie and Jeffrey Got Started

"Jeff and I went to Salem State College in Massachusetts," remembers Connie. "We were involved in theater programs there. We also had some excellent training in the high schools we went to—Jeff at Malden High, myself at Peabody High. When we graduated we were involved with Boston Globe Drama Festivals. We met during high school when he was performing at a festival and I was a judge. I had to disqualify him because his show went overtime. A year later we met again; we were both in the same class at college and we remembered each other.

"I've been in the business since I was a child. Dancing lessons at age 4, performing professionally by age 9. I had my own choreography company with which I supported myself through college.

"When we decided to do this, we looked around for a place to hold it. We've been on different cruises and in different hotels. You have to market yourself to the hotel and explain how this gimmick, so to speak, would enhance business for them.

"The Grosvenor decided to take a chance on us. Generally, we pull in 150 people on a Saturday night. Sometimes more, and then we do two shows back to back.

"We also do a lot of shows on the road; we've been flown to West Virginia and Puerto Rico, for example. We do a lot of convention work and other private parties."

The Finances Involved

"When we started in the beginning it was hard to function if we took just a cut. Some nights we'd get 150 people, some only 80," Connie says. "But we still had to pay the same expenses. We agreed to charge a flat fee. The fee can vary from hotel to hotel. We pay the actors and buy our own equipment. We also have our own liability insurance.

"Jeff still keeps his day job and I still have another part-time job. I work for the Disney University teaching an entertainment class. We take the students around to all the theme parks at Disney and use that as our classroom.

"MurderWatch has a lot of promise and it brings in enough to cover expenses, but it's not enough to support us right now. Nothing is easy in this business. We pay our performers on the night, but we don't always get paid on time.

"For everyone but myself, this is part-time work. The actors, musicians, and technicians are all independent contractors. The work is haphazard. There's no set schedule. We rotate through about 30 different actors, musicians, and technicians. We have five different shows we do, and each one uses between eight to ten performers. I'm the only official employee.

"It's not a lucrative venture to be in any end of theater. We try to pay our performers better than average—anywhere from $50 to $100 per performance. When we're on the road, we pay their traveling expenses.

"I write all the scripts. A lot of people do call us to see if they can write for us, but we tell them to contact the *Blue Sheet*. There are a lot of companies that look for scripts and they usually advertise in the *Blue Sheet*."

Some Tips from Connie

"Jeff and I have a lot of background in theater; we have a real solid knowledge," notes Connie. "A lot of other groups just have a bunch of actors that get together and say, 'Let's put on a show.' Unfortunately, they come and they go because they don't have solid business backgrounds. We have the business background. It is show *business*, after all.

"Jeff worked for eight years in a bank and is currently working as a logistics supervisor for a major corporation. I worked eight years as a computer analyst.

"You can't organize yourself and a group of people, especially people with egos, if you don't have a solid business background.

"I also think it's important not to try to do it all yourself. Have a team of people you can trust. It doesn't have to be a big team, it could be two or three people, like with us.

"In the theater everyone becomes close and like family, and it's fun to be able to keep that atmosphere like we do, but it is a business and you can't lose sight of that fact. If you do, and you get lax, you can fail.

"We have our long-term goals and we know where we're heading as a business. And the fun we have along the way is the fringe benefits. There's always a 'let's put on a show' atmosphere, but we never lose sight of the bottom line."

Freelance Writing

F reelance writing, which is the dream pursuit of many a self-starter, could easily be considered a service, but because it's such an extensive topic unto itself, it deserves an entire chapter. Freelance writers can find satisfying and financially rewarding work in one of two broad categories: writing for publication and writing for others. Related careers, such as fiction writing and working as a literary agent, can also be rewarding.

Writing for Publication

Visit any bookstore or newsstand and you will see hundreds of publications covering a variety of topics—from sports and cars to fashion and parenting. There are also many you won't see there, the hundreds of trade journals and magazines written for businesses, industries, and professional workers in as many different careers.

These publications all offer information on diverse subjects to their equally diverse readership. They are filled with articles and profiles, interviews and editorials, letters and advice, as well as pages and pages of advertisements. But without writers there would be nothing but advertisements between their covers—and even those are produced by writers!

Whether you work for a magazine full-time or as an independent freelancer, you will discover there is no shortage of markets where you can find work or sell your articles.

Differences between Staff Writers and Freelancers

A staff writer is employed full-time by a publication. She or he comes into work every day and is given article assignments to research and write or works with an editor to develop ideas.

A freelance writer works independently, in rented office space or in a home office. Most freelance writers plan and write articles and columns on their own and actively seek out new markets in which to place them.

Staff writers might have less freedom with what they choose to write, but they generally have more job security and always know when their next paycheck will arrive. Freelancers trade job security and regular pay for independence.

Both freelancers and those permanently employed have to produce high-quality work. They have editors to report to and deadlines to meet.

Different Kinds of Articles

Articles fall into two broad categories: those that educate and those that entertain. Here is just a small sampling of the topics magazine articles cover.

Art	Food
Aviation	Gardening
Business and finance	General interest
Careers	Health
Child care	Hobbies
Computers	Humor
Contemporary culture	Military
Entertainment	Nature

Pets	Retirement
Photography	Science
Politics	Sports
Psychology and self-help	Travel

Although the subject matter can be very different, most magazine articles include many of the same elements. They all start with an interesting "hook," that first paragraph that grabs the reader's (and the editor's) attention. They use quotes from real people, mention important facts, and sometimes include amusing anecdotes or experiences.

Getting That First Article Published

Freelance writers don't need a long, impressive resume to sell their first article. The writing will speak for itself.

Before starting, read as many magazines as you can, and in particular, those you would like to write for. It's never a good idea to send an article to a magazine you have never seen before. Being familiar with the different magazines will also help you come up with future article ideas.

Once you have decided what you want to write about, there are two ways you can proceed. You can write the entire article "on spec," send it off to appropriate editors, and hope they like your topic. Or first you can write a query letter, a kind of mini-proposal, to see if there is any interest in your idea. Query letters will save you the time of writing articles you might have difficulty selling. Only once you're given a definite assignment do you then proceed.

There are three important keys to keep in mind to get your articles published:

1. Make sure your writing is polished and that your article includes all the important elements.

2. Make sure your letter and manuscript are neatly typed and mistake-free.

3. Make sure you are sending your article to the right publication. A magazine that features stories only on planning the perfect wedding will not be interested in your piece on ten tips for the perfect divorce.

You can find out about different magazines and the kind of material they prefer to publish in the market guides listed in Appendix B.

The Finances Involved

Most writers are thrilled to see their "byline," that is, their name on the page, giving them credit for the article. And to writers, nothing is more exciting than the finished product, getting to see their stories in print.

Getting a check or a salary for your efforts can be rewarding as well, but sadly, for new freelancers, the checks might not come often enough and are not always large enough to live on.

While staff writers are paid a regular salary (though generally not a very high one), a freelancer gets paid only when he or she sells an article. Fees could range from as low as $5 to $1,000 or more depending on the publication. But even with a high-paying magazine, writers often have to wait until their story is published before they are paid. Because publishers work so far ahead, planning issues six months or more in advance, payment could be delayed from three months to a year or more.

To the freelancer's advantage, sometimes the same article can be sold to more than one magazine or newspaper. These "resales" help to increase salaries. And you can also be paid additional money if you can provide your own photographs to illustrate your articles.

Landing a Regular Column

Once a freelancer has become established, he or she can often land regular assignments with the same editors. This can even turn into a permanent column in a magazine or newspaper. A writer can even become syndicated, selling the same column to newspapers across the country.

A Garden Writer

When Robert (Bob) Haehle opens his daily mail, he's never quite sure what he'll receive. "This is the grimmer side of my job," Bob explains. "People send me dead leaves or bits of fruit and seeds. Sometimes I get squashed bugs. They have only three legs remaining and they were sent wrapped in plastic, so they're moldy and a terrible mess by the time I get them. You never know what's coming in the next load."

Bob is not the brunt of an harassment campaign; he writes a weekly question-and-answer format garden column for the *Fort Lauderdale Sun-Sentinel*, a newspaper with a circulation of more than 300,000. "I've developed a following. Readers cut out the columns and save them in scrapbooks. It's nice to know you're helping people."

Bob answers all questions that are sent to him: "Sometimes I have to play detective, to figure out what plants they're referring to; people use all sorts of different regional names. And, with certain problems, I can refer to my own garden. I have a collection of one of this or one of that—from a landscape point of view it might not always flow together that well, but as a study tool and a research tool, to know what's going on at any given time of the year, it's great to have all these things in the yard."

Questions range from how to protect backyard citrus trees from disease, to how to encourage blossoms from a bird-of- paradise. (For best results in the latter situation, Bob recommends allowing the family dog to help with the watering.)

"South Florida is a very special area," Bob says, "horticulturally different from the rest of the United States, with the exception of Hawaii. There really aren't a lot of gardening books dealing with all the conditions here. An incredible number of people move down here every year, but they're coming from different parts of the country and don't know what they're getting into. They may have gardened up north, but here you could almost literally say that conditions are 180 degrees different from the way they are in other locales. Up north it's acid soil; down here it's alkaline soil. Up north you plant your vegetables and annuals around May or so, and they're finished around October; here we plant them in October and usually get two crops, and then by April or May they're ready to pack it in. There are so many differences."

In addition to his column, Bob also regularly writes articles for the paper covering topics from roses and seashore gardening to storm-damage control and the proper pruning of trees.

He also freelances for a variety of regional magazines, such as *Florida Nurseryman* and *South Florida Home and Garden*, in addition to working with Time-Life garden encyclopedias.

The reason for all the activity, besides his love of what he's doing, is that it's difficult to make a living at freelance garden writing alone.

The Finances Involved

"I make about $100 a week for the column, maybe $150 for articles," Bob notes. "I enjoy writing, but only more or less when I feel like doing it. Someone more ambitious than I could probably make a full-time career out of it. They could work full-time on the staff of a paper, for example, but that's too structured for me."

How Bob Got Started

Bob is overly modest about his background, which is more than impressive. He has a bachelor's degree in environmental design/landscape architecture from the University of Massachusetts and a master's degree in horticulture and botanic garden management from the University of Delaware.

He has worked as an educational horticulturist at Brookside Gardens outside of Washington, DC, giving lectures and putting out a newsletter, and later as director of the facility. He took classes in horticultural writing during his master's program and also cohosted a radio phone-in show called "Plant Talk."

"You don't necessarily have to have a horticultural background to be a garden writer," acknowledges Bob, "but it does help. You should have a good background in English, and also have some interviewing skills for doing articles. It's also important to build up a good personal library of key reference books."

You can find Bob Haehle's column every Friday in the *Fort Lauderdale Sun-Sentinel*.

Writing for Others

There are many people, business owners or politicians, for example, who either because they do not have the skill or the time, hire the services of professional writers to do their writing for them.

You can keep busy writing magazine ads, travel brochures, political speeches, or press releases. The possibilities are as endless as the number of clients you can develop.

If you have an interest in writing, with a good command of English grammar, a grasp of the political process or knowledge of sales and marketing techniques—or you are willing to learn—then a career writing for others might be for you.

When you write for others, you either work in a client's or employer's office, or you can work from home as a freelance writer.

You will meet with your client or employer and listen to what he or she needs. Your project might be a brochure describing a resort hotel or a magazine ad to sell a new product.

You will then have to estimate the amount of time the job will take you, and what additional expenses, such as photography or art work, you will have. When you have calculated your time and the cost, you then give an exact price to the client. Even if your estimate was short and it takes you more time than you had initially planned, you still have to stick by your initial quote.

You most likely will be working on your own, and this means that you have to be self-motivated and disciplined. The client will want the project finished by a certain date and will expect you to deliver on time. That could mean you're working weekends and nights as well as days to get the job done.

What the Work Involves

When you write for others you could be involved in a variety of different projects. *Advertising copywriters* write all the words for magazine ads, and radio and television commercials. To describe a business's services or a client's product, they design and write the copy for brochures or pamphlets. They write all the copy for direct-mail packages, which are used to sell products or services, such as magazine subscriptions or memberships in a book club, through the mail.

Ghostwriters write books for people who don't have the necessary skills to do it themselves. The client could be a famous person such as a former president or a movie star who has a story to tell but needs help doing it. Ghostwriters sometimes get credit for their writing (you might see "as told to" on the book jacket cover), but many times they stay anonymous, writing behind the scenes.

Press secretaries work for government officials, actors and actresses, or big corporations that are concerned with relations with the press. They schedule public appearances and read prepared statements to reporters. They also write press releases that announce an event, a service, or a product. The press releases are sent to various newspapers and television and radio shows in the hopes of receiving some free publicity.

Speech writers work with politicians and other public figures, listening to what they want to say, then writing the speeches they will deliver. When you listen to the president on the television or see the mayor or governor speaking to a group of voters, you can make a good bet that the speech was written by someone else.

Finding Clients

Many writers work for ad agencies, gaining experience and making contacts before striking out on their own. Others might start with just one client, a big corporation, for example, that will send enough work their way. And, through building a reputation of being a good worker who delivers on time, you will receive recommendations from your clients, and that will lead you to new clients. Word of mouth is how most writers build up business.

The Finances Involved

In many careers, especially in the various areas of the writing profession, you'll hear the expression "the work is its own reward." What that means is the money you make doing that work isn't particularly exciting.

But, in the case of writing for others, the money can be as rewarding as the work.

Most people who write for others do it on a freelance basis. Although some charge a flat hourly rate, most charge by the project. It can be feast or famine starting out, but once you build a steady client base, your income can be very attractive.

There are a few writers who do earn a straight salary—press secretaries and writers working for advertising agencies. Salaries there can be anywhere from $25,000 a year for entry-level positions all the way up to $75,000 or more for experienced and successful employees.

The accompanying chart tells you what freelancers generally charge for a few selected projects.

	Hourly	Per Project
Advertising copywriting	$20–$100	$200–$4,000
Book-jacket copywriting		$100–$600
Brochures	$20–$50	$200–$4,000
Business catalogs	$25–$40	$60–$75 per printed page

Direct-mail package		$1,500–$10,000
Encyclopedia articles		$60–$80 per 1,000 words
Ghostwriting	$25–$100	$400–$25,000 or
		100% of the advance and
		50% of the royalties
Greeting cards		$20–$200 per verse
Press kits		$500–$3,000
Press releases		$80–$300
Speech writing	$20–$75	$100–$5,000
		(depending on the client)
Technical writing	$35–$75	$5 per page

Benefits of Freelancing

Independence is one of the pluses to writing for others, freelancers will tell you. For some jobs or projects, you can do your work in a home office, delivering the project when it's finished. You choose the projects you want to work on, and you set your own salary or fees.

The downside is that you have to learn how to promote yourself and seek out clients. In the beginning, you might have to call strangers on the phone or knock on office doors looking for work.

When you do have work, you'll also have deadlines. This means you'll have to deliver on time.

And some writers have a hard time asking for money. They would love to leave the business end of things to someone else. But when you write for others, you have to wear all the different hats. It's up to you to set the fee, draw up the invoices, and bill the client. It's also up to you to collect from the client if he or she happens to be late or seems as if he or she might not pay at all.

Rosalind Sedacca: Advertising Copywriter

Rosalind has been writing advertising copy for brochures, magazine ads, and television commercials for more than 15 years. She feels that it's important to always meet deadlines and to always give clients a little more than they're asking for. It's important that they feel they're getting their money's worth.

"I write ads for magazines, television and radio commercials, brochures, direct-mail packages, video scripts, newsletters, sales letters, and any other kind of material that needs to be written to help a company sell their product," explains Rosalind.

"When you write an ad, the first thing you have to know is what the purpose is. Then you want to understand who the market is, who will eventually be reading your writing. You have to understand the demographics—their age, their background, their sex, their income, their education level, and their interests.

If I'm writing a print ad for a teenage audience, I'm going to write it a lot differently from an ad for mothers or engineers.

"I work in tandem with other creative people who are graphic designers. I do the writing and the graphic designers take care of the layout and art. We team up and brainstorm; the words alone don't work unless they're placed on the page in attractive ways.

"The goal is to get people to visit, to buy, to subscribe, or to join. The products I write copy for include computers; hotels and resorts, such as Club Med; banks and real estate companies; car and appliance manufacturers; museums; magazines; all sorts of things."

One of the most interesting projects Rosalind has ever worked on is a new invention designed to detect counterfeit products: "There are so many forgeries in the world, it's become an international crisis. Unsuspecting buyers, thinking they are purchasing real Rolex watches or Reebok shoes, for example, might end up with very good fakes. Counterfeiters also print fake tickets for sporting events or theater shows, or fake money from countries around the world."

Rosalind's client is the inventor of a device that will help stop this problem. He has created a plastic decoder that when placed over a plastic strip on the product will show if it's genuine or not. Manufacturers can travel to different flea markets and shops to check for fake products. When the device is in place, they'll be able to read the words, "Genuine Reeboks" or "Genuine Currency." If those words don't appear, the manufacturers will know their products have been copied.

"My job was to write a detailed brochure describing this new invention and to also help set up a promotional tour," says Rosalind. "My client will soon be making appearances on '20/20' and other similar television shows."

How Rosalind Got Started

"I got started out of college wanting to work for *Vogue* magazine in the editorial department," she recalls. "I thought I wanted to work in the fashion world. I grew up in New York City and I went to [*Vogue*'s] personnel department, but they didn't have any openings. Instead, they offered me a position in advertising. I went to work as an assistant to the woman who was writing subscription letters, the ones you receive in the mail offering you subscriptions to different magazines.

"A year later, she left the company and I became creative director of circulation promotion for Condé Naste Publications, which owns *Vogue*, *Glamour*, *Mademoiselle*, *House and Garden*, and *Bride's*. It was a pretty cushy job for someone who was 21 years old. It inadvertently made me a direct-mail/advertising expert. I was with them for two years, then I left and moved into more general advertising for various advertising agencies in New York City, St. Louis, and Nashville. In 1984, I went out on my own and I've been independent since then."

What the Work Is Like

"It's very stimulating and creative," states Rosalind. "I never get bored; no two days are ever the same. What I like best, and what also can be a challenge, is that one minute I'm writing about a hotel, and the next minute I'm writing about a computer, and then I'm turning around and writing about a bank or about shoes. Sometimes it's hard to change mental gears to focus from one topic to another. It's the plus and the minus together.

"But I've got a perfect mix. Part of the week I'm in my home office working at the computer. I don't have to get dressed, no one sees me, I'm just on the phone a lot. The other part of the week I'm at meetings, either getting new clients or delivering my work, and then I'm dressed to the hilt and showing myself as a professional.

"The phone can take a lot of my time and I have to wear many hats. I do my own accounting and taxes, filing, all that administrative work such as sending bills to clients. I'd much rather be writing, but in a small business you have to do everything.

"And when you start out, the finances can be tricky at first. Feast or famine. But now it's smoothed out for me; I've been in business for a long time."

Becoming a Novelist

Fiction writers are creative, imaginative people. After all, they have to be; they make up stories for a living. Whether writing short stories or full-length novels, fiction writers have to be able to create imaginary characters and events and make them seem real to their readers.

Fiction writers have to be troublemakers, too, inventing all sorts of problems for their characters. They have to make their conversations and thoughts entertaining and fill their characters' lives with action. Finally, fiction writers have to be expert problem solvers, helping their heroes find satisfying solutions to their troubles by the end of the story.

If you love to read fiction and you find yourself stopping in the middle of a book and saying out loud, "I could do that better," then maybe you can.

The Writer's Life

Few new fiction writers have the luxury of working at their craft full-time—this applies to even the most dedicated of self-starters.

Most need to maintain some other sort of employment to help pay the bills until they are able to support themselves through their writing. Because of this, ambitious writers use every spare minute they have to work on their books or stories. John Grisham, for example, wrote a good deal of *The Firm* on yellow legal pads while taking the train to and from work as a full-time attorney in a law firm.

Others get up an hour earlier, stay up an hour later, turn down invitations to parties or other social events, or let the housework go—whatever they can do to find the time to write.

Successful authors who support themselves through their writing treat it as a full-time job. Most report learning how to discipline themselves to put in a certain number of hours each day.

Every writer chooses a schedule that is comfortable for him or her. Some work in the early hours of the morning, take afternoon naps, then go back to the computer in the evenings. Others write for eight or ten or twelve hours straight each day for a period of months until the book is finished. Still others might take years to complete one volume.

There is no set formula for how a writer should work. The only rule is that you have to write. Author James Clavell said that even if you write only one page every day for a year, at the end of that time you'll have 365 pages. And that's a good-size book.

The Many Categories of Fiction

Next time you visit a bookstore, take note of where the different books are shelved and what the signs in each section say. Here is an example of some of the different genres or categories you'll encounter, with a few of their subgenres also included.

General/mainstream

Action/adventure

Children's

Fantasy

Historical

Horror

Literary

Mystery
   Cozy
   Crime
   Detective
   Police procedural

Romance
   Contemporary
   Historical
      Gothic
      Regencies
   Sensuous
   Sweet

Science fiction

Suspense
   Psychological
   Woman-in-jeopardy

Thriller

Western

Young adult

Getting Your Novel Published

Writing a short story or a full-length novel is only half the battle. In addition to honing your skills as an expert storyteller, you also have to be a knowledgeable salesperson. That means you must learn which publishers you should approach and how to approach them. There are several market guides, which are mentioned in Appendix B, that tell you what categories of fiction different publishers buy.

The guides also list different magazines that purchase short stories. You can also check your own book collection to learn who publishes the books you read.

Once you've made a list of possible markets, you need to make sure your approach is appropriate. Your manuscript needs to be typed and double-spaced, with your name at the top of each page. There are several sources (also in Appendix B) that can give you the information you need to format your manuscript properly.

Before you send in your completed manuscript, you should write the editor a brief letter describing your project. Include a one-page synopsis or summary of your book's plot, and the first three chapters of your book as a sample. Don't forget to enclose a self-addressed stamped envelope (SASE). The editor will use this to send you a reply. If the editor likes what he or she sees, you'll probably receive a request to send more.

Alternatively, you can look for an agent first, following the same steps you'd use to make your initial approach to a publisher. But this time, you are asking that the agent consider you as a possible client.

At this point, after the query letters and sample chapters are in the mail, many new writers just sit back and wait for responses. The smart writer puts that manuscript out of his or her head and gets to work on the next one. And the next one. And the next one.

In the end, the key to getting published can be summed up in one word: persistence.

The Finances Involved

"Don't give up your day job just yet," is what the experts advise. Even if you manage to break in and sell your first novel, you should expect to receive only about $2,500 or $5,000.

The six-figure advances that some superstar authors receive are not the norm. Zebra Books senior editor John Scognamiglio says, "That kind of stuff like with John Grisham doesn't really have anything to do with the rest of us. There are 110,000 new titles a year, and there are only 15 on the *New York Times Bestseller List* at a time.

Most of the rest of us are going to make a moderate income and do a civilized business if we work very, very hard. There's not that much room at the top. And there isn't much of a middle class in publishing. You either make a little bit of money, which the grand majority will do, or you make a lot."

If you do manage to land that first book contract, you will receive an advance against royalties. A royalty is a percentage, usually 6 percent to 10 percent, of the money your book earns in sales. The advance is paid half on signing the contract, half on delivery and acceptance of the manuscript.

But money is not the only reason writers write. For some, the profession is almost an obsession—a burning desire to put words to paper, to start a book and see it to its finish. They wouldn't be happy doing anything else.

Other perks include recognition and publicity, although some might view the attention as a downside.

Many writers report that the nicest perk is being able to go to work in their bathrobe.

Joyce Sweeney: Young Adult Writer

Joyce Sweeney started sending her work to magazines and publishers when she was just 8 years old. She sold her first book when she was 18. Now, eight books later, Joyce still loves writing about adolescents; it's the time of life that fascinates her the most.

How Joyce Got Started

"I knew I wanted to be a writer all my life," she says. "I started writing when I was a kid and it made sense to be writing about other kids. But I didn't even know that the young adult (YA) genre existed. I was very ignorant about the whole thing.

"I would look through magazines to find the editors' address and send them a poem or something. I was used to rejections by the time I was a teenager. I didn't really know what I was doing, but the whole process made me feel good.

"Later, I wrote to agents and sent them samples of my work. Miraculously, I found an agent to represent me. She submitted *Center Line* to more than 30 publishers. I was getting pretty nervous, but I knew it was a good book. Then Delacorte Press held a contest for people who had never been published and I won first place. The prize was $5,000 and publication. All of my books have since been published by Delacorte.

"I write about whatever interests me at the moment. My readers are 10- to 14-year-olds. My book called *Shadow* is a ghost story, but it's also about sibling rivalry and domestic violence. Another book is an adventure story about four boys trapped in a cave. I've written about suicide and homosexuality, too."

The Difficulties Involved

"When I was a kid, YA novels were not that great," remembers Joyce. "They were formula books that I didn't associate with quality. Then, I realized that this was a market niche where you could write high-quality fiction, and it wasn't so tough to get published. For me, it was a nice way to be true to myself.

"But it does get more and more competitive every year. The series books are giving us a hard time. The bookstores tend to buy *The Babysitter's Club* and nothing else. If you are writing ordinary mainstream books, it's getting harder and harder.

"Also, I find it a little difficult to market myself, at least locally. If I go to a children's event, the kids there are too young for my books. If I go to an event with adult authors, no one there is really interested.

"And just being a writer is a constant struggle. It's difficult to write, it's difficult to keep writing. You know you could make more money in advertising.

"I've started books and found out that they were going nowhere and had to throw them out. I haven't had too many bad reviews, but I've had books that I thought were great that didn't sell that well. My second book, for example. There are ups and downs all the time.

"A big thing that happens to me a lot, though it doesn't sound much like a downside, is that I get approached by the movies a lot, to have my books made into feature films or television movies. But it never quite happens. They just get dropped.

"It's not a steady, calm sort of work. There's the unpredictability of sales and the market, the unpredictability of whether I'm writing something good at a given moment. I'm never sure if the next book will be okay, as good as the one before it."

On the Plus Side

"I think children are a more appreciative audience than adults," Joyce notes. "I go to schools, and I find I have real fans out there. They're excited and enthusiastic, they write letters to me. I can really see that I'm having an effect. I think back to when I was a kid, and I know that the books they read at that age make a huge difference. It can change their whole life or influence them this way or that way. It's exciting to be able to touch someone at that particular age.

"I never get tired of that. This is where I belong."

Some Advice from Joyce

"Read as much as you possibly can, and read the authors you would like to be like. Try to pick up as much as you can about writing that way," recommends Joyce.

"Find out if there are any creative writing classes or programs available to you and enroll.

"And no matter how young you are, you should send things out, just for the practice and to get used to rejection slips."

Self-Publishing

For those writers whose books don't meet conventional publishing criteria—the topic or the audience are too narrow to make marketing the book cost-effective, for example—and who feel they can reach their audience by themselves, self-publishing might be the route to go.

The self-publisher sets up his or her own publishing company and controls every facet of production, promotion, and distribution. The financial outlay is the complete responsibility of the self-publisher. But in return, all profits, if there are any, go to the self-publisher.

Undertaking a self-publishing book project is a big step. It involves a lot of time and money, and the self-publisher needs to have a variety of skills in addition to writing ability. In self-publishing, marketing and promotional expertise are more important than being able to write.

The Finances Involved

Depending on how many copies of a book you print, the outlay could be anywhere from $5,000 to $15,000. When deciding how much to charge for your book, you need to remember that, unless you have a ready-made retail audience for the book, most of your sales will go to distributors, libraries, or bookstores. For those markets you will receive only 40 percent to 60 percent of the retail cost of your book.

Two Pitfalls to Avoid

1. Don't overprint. Your first run should be no more than 2,000 copies. See if there's a market for your work before you fill up your living room or garage with cartons of books.

2. Stay away from self-publishing fiction. Self-published books can be very difficult to sell—with fiction it borders on the impossible. Most self-published books carry an automatic stigma: Why wasn't it good enough for a legitimate publisher to take on? Some nonfiction books can avoid that stigma; most fiction can't.

Tom Bernardin:
Author of *The Ellis Island Immigrant Cookbook*

Tom Bernardin worked as a seasonal employee for three years for the National Park Service at Ellis Island.

"Ellis Island is part of the Statue of Liberty National Monument," Tom explains. "They're two separate islands but they're right beside each other.

"I had originally hoped to land a job on the maintenance staff at the Statue of Liberty. I wanted to cut grass. The woman who interviewed me and later became my boss took a look at my application and saw that I had a college degree and was a teacher of English as a second language to recent immigrants. She wanted me on her interpretive staff at Ellis Island. I was aware of the position but at the time I'd had my public speaking experience only from teaching and I was a bit nervous. Still, I just knew that I'd like it. I'd always been interested in Ellis Island, it's so loaded with history. It opened in 1975 for visitors and I had hoped to be on the first tour boat, but I was teaching that day.

"I took the job and had absolutely no regrets. The best part of my job was having access to Ellis Island and becoming a part of its history, making the public aware of how important it was, tapping into the emotions visitors brought with them."

Although it has been two decades since Tom Bernardin left his job at Ellis Island, the monument is still very much with him. In 1981 Tom developed a slide lecture called "Ellis Island: The Golden Door," and in 1991 self-published his book, *The Ellis Island Immigrant Cookbook*. As well as recipes contributed by immigrants and their descendants, the pages are filled with heartwarming, and at times heartwrenching, accounts of the Ellis Island experience.

Tom had two ready-made markets when he undertook to compile his book: the gift shops at both the Statue of Liberty and Ellis Island. Tom also regularly tours the country speaking to different groups about the rich history of Ellis Island. To date he has sold more than 30,000 copies of his book.

Becoming a Literary Agent

Perhaps you'd prefer to be on the other side of the desk, so to speak, helping writers get published, rather than writing yourself.

The Role of the Literary Agent

Literary agents act as go-betweens for writers and editors. These days most of the big New York publishing houses refuse to consider manuscripts unless they are sent in by an agent. Many publishers credit agents with the ability to screen out inappropriate submissions. An agent is expected to be familiar with the different kinds of books publishers prefer to take on.

An agent spends his or her time reading manuscripts, choosing which ones to work with, and then trying to sell them to publishers. Agents free a writer to concentrate on writing instead of marketing. The agent's job is to find the right house for a client's work and, once successful, to negotiate the best financial deal for the writer. Agents also handle film rights for feature or television movies and foreign rights, selling books to publishers overseas.

How Literary Agencies Are Structured

Some literary agents choose to work on their own, with little more than secretarial assistance. They can rent space in an office building or work from a home office.

Other agents prefer to work within a literary agency, either as the owner or as one of the associates. They can still function independently, choosing the writers and book projects they want to work with. Usually, in an agency agents must contribute a percentage of their income to cover the office's operating expenses.

Training for Agents

Most agents have at least a bachelor's degree, although not necessarily in English. Any liberal arts or humanities major, in addition to writing and literature courses, will provide the necessary background. It is also helpful to be familiar with publishing law and contracts, and to know how to type or use a word processor.

Most skills can be learned through on-the-job experience but, as with writers, agents should also be avid readers.

The Finances Involved

Agents must sell their clients' manuscripts to publishers in order to earn any income. Agents generally work on a commission basis, 10 percent to 15 percent of the money the writer earns. If an agent has a lot of market savvy, carefully chooses which manuscripts to represent, and has success bargaining for big advances and royalty percentages, he or she can make a very good living, often much more than the editors to whom he or she is selling.

The downside for agents is that the marketplace is fickle, fads come and go, publishing houses merge with each other and often decrease the number of books they will print. In a bad year, an agent can often have to struggle to make a living.

Nancy Yost: Literary Agent

Nancy Yost started out as a contract editor at Random House, then moved to Avon Books and worked there as an editor from 1986 to 1990. Now she is one of three full-time agents at Lowenstein Associates, Inc., in New York City who together represent more than 150 writers of fiction and nonfiction.

"Publishing houses are organized by lists—they have certain kinds of books they're good at, and they have certain kinds of books they don't do," says Nancy. "For example, Avon is very good with romances, very good with original mysteries, they have great science fiction and fantasy editors. But if you ever wanted to work with a big picture book or a cookbook, you couldn't. You were limited by the list. It seemed to me that if I became an agent I'd be able to play in everyone's backyard instead of just one.

"And the money is better, of course; the more you sell, the more you earn. And you only work with the people you want to work with. Even in the best of publishing houses you have salespeople, marketing people, production people, who are all many times at odds with your vision of a book or your enthusiasm for a book. The only limit on my enthusiasm now is what I think the market can do. If one publisher doesn't like it, I can go to 6 others—or 20 others—until I sell it or until I've been beaten down and realize I'm not going to be able to sell it.

"The job is very busy. I carry 50 clients at any one time. That's not to say I am always trying to sell 50 new manuscripts at once. Each of my writers produces one to two books a year, and my time is easily manageable.

"I like to work with narrative nonfiction—true crime, science books, human interest stories, offbeat humor titles—and commercial fiction, including contemporary women's novels and mysteries.

"I receive a lot of submissions every week—query letters and complete manuscripts. How I approach my submissions is in the nature of triage. The ones that are going to die, I have to reject right away, the ones that I'm really excited about, I ask to see more right away. The ones that look as if there might be something there, but don't really stand out, tend to sit the longest. The converse of that is being sent something that's really good, but I'm too busy with other commitments at the time—sometimes I have trouble finding a chunk of time to set aside to devote to it.

"Once I have received a presentable manuscript," she explains, "I talk to editors on the phone before I send it out. It gives me a chance to feel them out, and it also gives me a chance to express my enthusiasm for the project.

"I'm always excited when a manuscript comes in that has quality—style, voice, fresh thinking. But a manuscript needing a lot of editing work won't interest me. It won't be worth my while to take something like that on unless it's perfectly fabulous and I can see major money for it.

"Part of me always cringes when I have to reject a manuscript I have no interest in. But if I'm not the right person to handle it, it's better the writer knows right away.

"And sometimes there's a problem with rude writers and messy manuscripts. Once in awhile an attitude comes through that puts you off."

For More Information

Books and professional associations of interest to writers and potential agents are listed in Appendices A and B.

CHAPTER SIX

The Organizer

Not only are you a self-starter, you're an organized one. You make to-do lists for all your activities, and you even keep track of them and check off entries as they are completed. You have the knack of being able to pull people together for an event or special occasion. If a party needs to be planned and catered, a seminar orchestrated, a luncheon meeting organized, you're the person at the helm, controlling all the various elements.

You pay attention to details, you can juggle different tasks at the same time, and, as the day draw nears, you not only watch everything fall into place, you make sure it does.

What can a self-starter do with these valuable skills? Many such as yourself channel their abilities into organizing some of the following events:

Seminars

Workshops

Conventions

Conferences

Weddings

Parties

Associations

Collectives

Clubs

Speakers' bureaus

How to Get Started

The self-employed organizer first needs to see a need or develop one. If you're a writer, you can organize seminars; if you're a plant lover you can arrange for garden exhibitions; if you're a photographer, you can put on a community photography competition. You can also contact existing groups—writers' associations, historical associations, the chamber of commerce, to name just a few—and let them know of your services.

Each event or organization has its own particular requirements. Here are some of the details an organizer might have to attend to:
- Raising financing
- Arranging for a venue, such as a conference hall, hotel ballroom, or school gym
- Hiring speakers or entertainment
- Catering refreshments
- Designing, writing, printing, and distributing promotional material
- Renting equipment or furnishings
- Keeping track of registrations or guest lists
- Sending confirmation letters
- Allocating seating
- Arranging for accommodations
- Arranging for transportation

This chapter provides a few examples of successful projects for organizers.

Starting an Association

Do you have an avid interest or hobby, or an unusual occupation for which there seems to be little professional support, especially in your specific location? If so, you can start your own membership organization or professional association. That's what Dana Cassell did almost 15 years ago.

To begin with, Dana is a freelance writer. She's had more than 1,200 magazine articles and columns appear in 150+ consumer, business, and trade magazines, including *Modern Bride*, *Mother Earth News*, *The Single Parent*, *Teens & Boys*, *Women's Circle*, *Working Woman*, *The Writer*, and *Writer's Digest*. She is also director and founder of Cassell Network of Writers (CNW), an organization with more than 1,000 members.

"After working for almost 10 years building up a client base, getting to know editors and other writers I met at conferences, I realized that these two groups sometimes had difficulty finding each other," explains Dana. "That's how the idea for CNW was born.

"With the goal in mind to act as a link between editors and writers and to provide information to writers to enable them to be more successful, I tested the market to see what the interest level was. After a positive response to my initial mailing, I did a bigger mailing. I attracted 300 members the first year; membership has now grown to well over 1,000.

"CNW was a natural outgrowth of that basic profession of being an independent writer. I always thought I would keep writing and that CNW would be just a sideline. But it grew and grew and took over, becoming the main focus.

"I expect I will always write," she continues. "When I 'retire,' I will just divest myself of the other parts of the business.

"I love the freedom of being my own boss, the excuse to talk to anybody about anything while doing research, the continual use of books and libraries and magazines, the ability to work at home— which I love—seeing my byline (one never gets tired of that), the satisfaction that information I communicate via workshops and seminars has helped a writer become successful.

"But, as satisfying as that is, I'm not sure that it quite equals what it's like to come up with an idea for an article or book, follow it through, and have someone else publish it with your name on it.

"When I do take time off, the work (mail, especially) continues to pile up and deadlines loom closer, so I have to work twice as hard when I return—which is the major reason I don't take lengthy vacations.

"Also, the financial insecurity. We all dream of a best-seller. I'd probably still work as hard and as long, but it would be nice to eliminate the 'will-enough-money-come-in-this-week-to-pay-the-bills' syndrome.

"And because CNW has so many members, I have less time to write now."

How Dana Got Started

"Because of my high school journalism class and work on the school paper, I was able to get a job on a small-town weekly newspaper," she recalls. "The editor subscribed to *Writer's Digest*. I learned through this magazine that ordinary people (like me!) could write articles and have them published in magazines. It opened a whole new world for me.

"After several years of studying and practicing, I became a real, published freelance writer and discovered that this was what I was happiest doing. I could never get completely away from it, even when I tried to."

What CNW Is

Cassell Network of Writers is a membership organization of writers wanting to learn more about their craft, how to get published more regularly, how to take care of the business side of freelancing. Dana produces an information-packed newsletter each month, with writing and business tips, market listings for articles, contests for writers, and a calendar of events such as seminars and workshops.

She has organized all-day seminars and three- and four-day state-wide writers' conferences, bringing in speakers—published authors, editors, and agents—from all over the country.

She also runs a member referral service, connecting freelancers with anyone who requires the services of a writer. In addition, she operates a toll-free hotline to field questions from members.

A Typical Day for Dana

8:00–8:15	File reference material.
8:15–10:00	Make additions to my book manuscript (*The Encyclopedia of Obesity and Eating Disorders*).
10:00–10:20	Go to the post office.
10:20–11:00	Open and sort mail; log in income.
11:00–2:30	Go to the printer to pick up material for membership direct-mail package; drop off mailing materials to the person who will do the labeling and stuffing; go to the bank to make end-of-month deposits; stop at the Salvation Army store to look for any used books of interest.
2:30–3:00	Return phone calls from CNW members.
3:00–4:30	Complete manuscript work started earlier; take several phone calls; skim a few magazines; brainstorm ideas for new articles.
4:30–5:30	Dinner.
5:30–5:45	"Clean up" work to computer mailing list (we now have a list of 26,000 writers).
5:45–6:45	Work on a writing project.
6:45–7:15	Do some reading on time management.
7:15–7:45	Work on a marketing plan for my books.
7:45–8:40	Update information on the computer (seminar and conference registrations, membership applications, book orders).
8:40–9:15	Catalog personal CD collection.
9:15–12:00	Print out mailing labels for the state conference.
12:00–12:30	Install a new software program.
12:30–12:45	Plan next day's tasks.
12:45–	Good night.

Starting a Collective
Moosewood Restaurant

Moosewood Restaurant, in Ithaca, New York, opened its doors in 1973 as a collectively run vegetarian eating establishment. Part of the counterculture at the time, Moosewood workers were early adherents to the now-popular philosophy that food could be healthful and taste good at the same time. They also felt that the workplace should be a fun place to be, with all business decisions made jointly.

At present, 18 women and men rotate through the jobs necessary to make a restaurant run, planning menus, setting long-term goals—and washing pots. Their ranks are bolstered by about half a dozen employees.

Most of the Moosewood collective have worked together for over ten years; several since the restaurant's early days.

Moosewood was at first known only locally. Now, two decades and several highly acclaimed cookbooks later, Moosewood's reputation for serving fine food in a friendly atmosphere has spread nationally.

And they have not lost sight of their original philosophy. Moosehead is still owned and run collectively, and still serves quality meals at reasonable prices.

David Hirsch joined the Moosewood collective in 1976. He started as a waiter/busboy but soon took on the responsibilities of chef and menu planner. He is also the author of *The Moosewood Restaurant Kitchen Garden* and co-author of three other books— *New Recipes from Moosewood Restaurant, Sundays at Moosewood Restaurant,* and *Moosewood Restaurant Cooks at Home.*

David earned his bachelor of architecture degree in 1968 at City College of New York. He worked in various architectural firms for a few years before moving to Ithaca.

Making a Collective Work

Collectives have come and gone over the years; it takes a lot of different elements to make one work. If this is a career path that intrigues you, these tips from David can point you in the right direction: "To start a successful collective, just like with any business, you first must judge the need, do some market research. Are people clamoring for this business to serve them?

"Then you have to gather capital. Look for a guardian angel or a potential collective member with a trust fund!

"Banks are unlikely to immediately loan money to a business with no collateral. They might loan to individuals who can put up their homes, take a second mortgage—put their own capital on the line or that of a friend or relative. But banks are wary about putting their money down without having something to hold on to.

"With Moosewood, an enormous amount of money wasn't necessary. We started with a small space and bought some secondhand equipment.

"Someone in the collective should also have some business background; if not, you need to be prepared to hire someone who does.

"Specifically in the restaurant business, you need to be able to work under pressure. So many restaurants go under. Moosewood has been around all these years because we continue to look for interesting international recipes that please our customers. And our timing was right.

"And, obviously, in a worker/manager situation, you need to be somehow connected to other people who have similar interests. You can't do it yourself; you need good support, a network of people you trust. We didn't put an ad in the paper looking for collective members. Moosewood is unique, a network of connected friends and acquaintances that grew in a fairly organic way."

Twenty years ago, the times were different. But a collective is still a possibility—if the variables *can* be jelled. Employees *can* be the owners of their businesses. In fact, there are stories coming from everywhere about employers selling their businesses back to the employees.

"Once you are involved, try to create situations that can expand your interest in whatever you want to do so it doesn't get stale. Look for something that really excites you, interests you. You have to be comfortable with it. If you find yourself watching the clock wishing you were out of there, then you really probably should be out of there.

"Being a part of a collective involves commitment. With a more traditional job, you can just go home at the end of the day. With a collective, there are meetings to attend and responsibilities to share. You have to be willing to do that."

Getting a Foot in the Door

"We occasionally take on new members," says David. "To be a part of Moosewood, we'd have to see a resume, but we tend to hire people we can interview on a personal basis. We work very closely together in a small space.

"Write first, then if we like what we see, you'd need to come up. To get a foot in the door, it's a good idea to take a few cooking courses, though there are not very many that specialize in just vegetarian cuisine. Various culinary institutes or some community colleges or adult education programs might offer appropriate courses.

"At Moosewood, nobody starts off right away as a chef. You need to gain some experience here, to have the repertoire down. We start our new members off slowly, working with someone more senior at the beginning, as an extra cook on a shift. And, of course, we also have recipes written down to follow.

"My desire to leave the city and join the back-to-the-land movement brought me to Ithaca in 1972," he recalls. "I spent a couple of years building a house in the country, then, to earn some money, I got a job as a cook for a couple of different fraternities at Cornell University. I could have summers off and could devote time to other pursuits. My interest in architecture was replaced with my love of the earth, gardening, hiking, and the out-of-doors.

"But I discovered I also loved to cook. It's fun and direct; the results are immediate.

"I got hooked up with Moosewood, by then in its third year, though at the time I wasn't thinking about a long-term career. I was disgruntled with the atmosphere cooking at the fraternities and wanted to be with people who shared my values. Moosewood was the perfect place."

David's Duties at Moosewood

David divides his time between cooking, planning menus, ordering food and supplies, testing recipes for the books, writing, attending meetings, and occasionally waiting on tables.

Because of the Moosewood cookbooks, he also occasionally is involved in book promotions, attending local booksignings, and appearing on television and radio shows. He also does some catering and consulting and teaches hands-on cooking workshops.

The Finances Involved

"At Moosewood, our priorities have always had a lot to do with how we feel about the workplace, and not about amassing great fortunes," notes David. "With so many people involved sharing dividends, income gets watered down, even with a large book advance.

"The reasons to be in our collective have to be heartfelt. Rewards could be strongly financial in another type of collective or business venture, but not necessarily so. It depends on the market, where you are, what service or product you are providing.

"In a restaurant collective, financial rewards are far from glamorous. Entry-level salaries start somewhere in the teens. With three or four years of experience, someone might make $20,000 or so, depending on how many hours a week he or she chooses to work."

The Hours Involved

"Most traditional restaurant owners would probably have to work 60 to 70 hours a week," says David. "One advantage of a collective is you can work fewer hours if you choose."

The Upside

"From the very beginning, I really liked Moosewood," he remembers. "It felt different to me from any other job. There's no hierarchy, you're working with peers. There are built-in checks and balances, no authority figures to say, 'You have to do it this way because I say so.' Everyone's on equal ground.

"The atmosphere is supportive, rather than competitive. You don't have a group of people vying for a vice presidency or the next upper position.

"There's a more honest approach on a daily basis. It's all very appealing, direct. You go in, make the food, and people appreciate it. This is something I can care about. I feel good about what I'm doing."

The Downside

"What I like least is dealing with the push and pull from all the different directions, the different people," admits David. "The collective process working towards consensus can be frustrating at times."

You can write to Moosewood for more information at the address given in Appendix A.

Finger Lakes Organic Growers Cooperative

The Finger Lakes Organic Growers is a cooperative enterprise with approximately thirty active members. Most of the farms, which are spread across New York State, are 15 acres or smaller. All growers have purchased shares in the cooperative, and the cooperative in exchange markets their produce for them.

Their aim is to grow all their crops organically without the use of any chemical pesticides or fertilizers. They are committed to sustainable agriculture, meaning they farm in such a way that the environment benefits from it—the soil gets richer and the general ecology is preserved.

Carol Stull is one of the founding members of the Finger Lakes Organic Growers Cooperative, which began operation in 1986. "It actually started under the black locust tree in my backyard," Carol explains. "There had been a group of growers, about six of us, that had been meeting and talking about how running around and trying to sell everything ourselves was a hassle. Several of our regular customers would buy one thing from someone, but if they ran out, they'd go to someone else. So our thinking was that if we could go together, it would be more expeditious.

"We had been talking about it for a year and then one of the growers said, 'Let's do it and here's my $5 to start.' We used that to mail out the minutes. Then we applied for a grant from New York State Agriculture and Markets. At the time, they had money they'd gotten from the federal government for grants.

"We got $15,000 and we used it as start-up money for the co-operative. We set up a computer program, and we rented a truck for deliveries. The market manager worked out of her living room then. That first year we didn't even have a warehouse—we used a farm that belonged to one of our growers, and we brought things there or to a couple of pickup points. We were pretty low-budget, but we were able to pay an artist to develop our logo and to get office supplies. And also, when you sell things, there's a delay between the time you sell and the time you get the money, so we used some of the grant to cover employees' salaries.

"Each member has his own farm. Right at the beginning, one of the things we decided is that we couldn't compete with each other in the marketplace. We got advice from a Vista volunteer who worked with another cooperative, and learned that we should, for example, set up a personnel committee so every grower wasn't telling the manager something different to do. We each gave up all our wholesale markets to the co-op. It used to cost us at least a quarter of our time to do the selling, and that really wasn't enough to do it right. So we've changed that now, and the manager takes care of all of that."

Carol's Individual Farm

Carol and her husband bought their land in Ithaca, New York, in 1985. "Our business was only a year old when we started the co-operative," she remembers. "Before that we used to market our produce direct at farmer's markets. We were small, just learning to go from packets to pounds. You buy a packet of seeds for a small home garden, but when you're growing commercially you buy seeds by the pound. We have 65 acres and farm about 10 acres of it. We grow all of the standard vegetables, except corn. We have a problem with deer.

"One of the reasons I like doing this is that I can grow any weird thing I want. That was one of our entries into the wholesale restaurant market. I can grow edible flowers or unusual cherry tomatoes that other people don't grow. We also grow a lot of herbs—seven or eight different basils, for example.

"The number of employees I have fluctuates. In the summer I hire students. We have about eight who help with the planting and picking. It's a lot easier if you have several thousand tomato plants and six or eight people to chat with as you're picking. Then it can be fun work. By yourself, it's a lot harder.

"I do all the planning. We grow a lot of different crops, so we have to know where they're going to go. We do a three-year rotation, which means we don't plant crops from the same family in the same place in the field for three years.

"There's a lot of planning and a lot of adjusting to your planning if things don't work out—whether it's the weather that doesn't co-operate, or the equipment breaks down, or someone doesn't show up, or things grow faster or slower than you thought they would. You spend a lot of time figuring out what you're doing. We have 187 different food products and a wide line of perennials and herb plants, and that's a lot going on.

"We have three greenhouses, and in the winter I grow a lot of salad greens for the hotel school at Cornell."

Carol also sells at the local farmer's market on Saturdays and has a roadside stand on her property. "When you have more cherry tomatoes than you absolutely know what to do with, you look at every market available."

Carol's Background

Carol was trained as a clinical chemist with a biology background, and she worked eighteen years as a hospital chemist. Her bachelor's degree is from the University of Illinois; her master's is from Baylor in Texas.

Although she grew up in suburban Evanston, Illinois, there's been a farm in her family since her great-grandfather's time.

Carol loves farming. "We have a very inspiring view. Our farm sits on top of a hill overlooking twenty miles of Cayuga Lake. If you're feeling a little down in the morning, the view will perk you up," she says.

"But what I like most is the fascination of seeing a little seedling transfer into something big, watching the flowers open up. Then seeing the fruits of your labor when you go out and start harvesting. The little plants you transplanted are now ready to be eaten or sold or whatever you're going to do with them. It's a thrill."

The Finances Involved

Income for farmers can vary from year to year. Food prices fluctuate from week to week and are affected by the weather and other factors that influence the demand for certain products. The size and type of the farm also affects income. Generally, large farms produce more income than smaller operations. The exception to that are specialty farms producing small amounts of high-value horticultural and fruit products.

According to the U.S. Department of Agriculture, average income after expenses for operators of vegetable and fruit farms was $100,000 in 1993. Individual income can vary widely. Sally Miller, the manager of the Finger Lakes Organic Growers, earns $8.25 an hour; her assistant manager started out at $6.50 an hour and will go up to $7 or $7.50 after she's been on board for awhile.

Carol Stull's seasonal workers earn between minimum wage and about $5 an hour. The growers within the cooperative earn different amounts depending on the size of their property or what kind of year they have. The earnings could range from just $1,000 to about $35,000 or $40,000 gross sales. Carol's own farm grosses about $25,000 to $30,000 a year. "People don't realize how much it costs people to grow food," Carol says. "I'm still selling things at the same price I was ten years ago because that's what people expect to pay. But ten years ago the minimum wage was lower; now it's gone up and I pay workman's comp and social security, too.

"It's what I do for a living, but my husband also has a full-time job outside the farm. I wouldn't be able to do this at this level if it were just me. As you pay off your equipment and mortgage, you have a little more left over for your own salary, but it's not easy."

Because the work for some farmers and managers is seasonal, and the income fluctuates so, many growers take second jobs during the off months.

Professional Associations

Dream Schemes

Contact the following professional associations for more information about the floral industry:

Jim Behrens, Director of
  Educational Programs
American Floral Services, Inc.
PO Box 12309
Oklahoma City, OK 73157

American Floral Art School
529 South Wabash Ave, #600
Chicago, IL 60605-1679

American Florists Association
2525 Heathcliff
Reston, VA 22091

American Institute of Floral
  Designers
720 Light Street
Baltimore, MD 21230-3816

Society of American Florists
1601 Duke Street
Alexandria, VA 22314-3406

For information about Herrell's Ice Cream franchises, contact Steve Herrell at:

Herrell's
8 Old South Street
Northampton, MA 01060

Service Industry Careers

Lists of barber schools, by state, are available from:

National Association of Barber Schools, Inc.
304 South 11th St.
Lincoln, NE 68502

A list of licensed training schools and licensing requirements for cosmetologists can be obtained from:

National Accrediting Commission
  of Cosmetology Arts and Sciences
901 North Stuart St., Suite 900
Arlington, VA 22203

Association of Accredited
  Cosmetology Schools, Inc.
5201 Leesburg Pike
Falls Church, VA 22041

Information about barber and cosmetology schools also is available from:

Accrediting Commission of Career
  Schools/Colleges of Technology
750 1st St. NE, Suite 905,
Washington, DC 20002

For details on state licensing requirements and approved barber or cosmetology schools, contact the state board of barber examiners or the state board of cosmetology in your state capital.

For information on training and certification for a career as a personal trainer, contact the following associations:

American Council on Exercise (ACE)
PO Box 910449
San Diego, CA 92191
(Provides certification for personal
  trainers)

Orthopedic Certification Board
  (ONCB)
Box 56
East Holly Avenue
Pitman, NJ 08071

American College of Sports
  Medicine (ACSM)
Member and Chapter Services
  Department
PO Box 1440
Indianapolis, IN 46206

International Physical Fitness
  Association
415 W. Court Street
Flint, MI 48503

For information on becoming an auctioneer, contact:

National Auctioneers Association
8880 Ballentine
Overland Park, KS 66214

For more information on genealogy, contact:

Accreditation Program
Family History Library
35 N. West Temple Street
Salt Lake City, UT 84150

Board for Certification of
    Genealogists
PO Box 5816
Falmouth, VA 22403-5816

Careers for Performers

For information on the Art Deco District, the January weekend, or hotel reservations, contact:

Miami Design Preservation League
PO Box Bin L
Miami Beach, FL 33119

A Way with Words

American Society of Journalists and
    Authors
1501 Broadway
New York, NY 10036

Garden Writers Association of
    America
c/o Robert La Gasse
10210 Leatherleaf Court
Manassas, VA 22111

Association of Authors
    Representatives (AAR)
10 Astor Place, 3rd Floor
New York, NY 10003

The Organizer

Institute for Alternative Agriculture
9200 Edmonton Road, Suite 117
Greenbelt, MD 20770

Moosewood Restaurant
215 North Cayuga Street
Ithaca, NY 14850

APPENDIX B

Recommended Reading

Dream Schemes

For more information on operating your own bed-and-breakfast establishment, the following two books will be helpful:

How to Start and Run a Bed & Breakfast Inn by Ripley Hotch and Carl Glassman, Stackpole Books. Covers buying the right inn, attracting guests, estimating costs and profitability.
The Seventh Old House Catalog by Lawrence Grow, Sterling/Main Street Publishing. An A-to-Z sourcebook for restoration and remodeling.

The following publications will give you insight into horticultural careers:

Careers for Plant Lovers by Blythe Camenson, VGM Career Horizons.
Opportunities in Horticulture Careers by Jan Goldberg, VGM Career Horizons.
PFD—Professional Floral Design, Floral Finance, and *Retail Florist,* three monthlies available through AFS, PO Box 12309, Oklahoma City, OK 73157.

Careers for Performers

For information on the entertainment industry, including acting opportunities, contact the *Florida Blue Sheet.* Although a local publication, it is read nationally:

Florida Blue Sheet
7238 Hiawassee Oak Drive
Orlando, FL 32818-8360

The following books may give you some ideas of what to include in a walking tour:

Mystery Reader's Walking Guide: New York, Alzina Dale, Passport Books.
Mystery Reader's Walking Guide: England by Alzina Dale and Barbara Sloan Hendershott, Passport Books.
Mystery Reader's Walking Guide: London by Alzina Dale and Barbara Sloan Hendershott, Passport Books.

A Way with Words

Guide to Literary Agents and Art/Photo Reps, available annually from Writer's Digest Books.
How to Write a Book Proposal by Michael Larsen, Writer's Digest Books, 1985.
How to Write Irresistible Query Letters by Lisa Collier Cool, Writer's Digest Books, 1987.
Writer's Market, available annually from Writer's Digest Books.
Ellis Island Immigrant Cookbook by Tom Bernardin, 175 Fifth Avenue, Suite 2306, New York, NY 10010

For $1 (send a check, not cash), you can purchase a helpful report on self-publishing titled *Should You Pay to Have It Published?* from Writer's Digest Books, 1507 Dana Avenue, Cincinnati, OH 45207. Writer's Digest Books also publishes the *Complete Guide to Self-Publishing* by Tom and Marilyn Ross. This entrepreneurial couple self-published six books. The knowledge they picked up along the way led to the creation of their consulting service which regularly helps authors self-publish. (You will notice, however, that their very successful guide to self-publishing was *not* self-published!)